DRAFT, REGISTRATION
and THE LAW

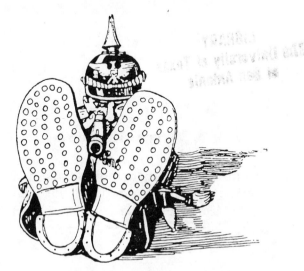

A Guidebook
by R. CHARLES JOHNSON
Attorney and Draft Counselor

Editor: Charles E. Sherman

NOLO PRESS

PO Box 544, Occidental, CA 95465

Dedication

dedicated to
millions of young men
and to those who care about them

Acknowledgements

Some of the information used in this book was taken from materials produced by the Central Committee for Conscientious Objectors. Then again, some of the CCCO materials used were written by me. It all evens out.

Thanks to Los Angeles attorney William G. Smith, San Francisco draft counselors Stephen Huston and Janet Cronbach, and Marin County draft counselors Burt Greene and Ann Spake, for their valuable comments.

Special thanks to David Whyte for his thoughts on draft registration, and to Cedric Wentworth for the information on conscientious objection in other countries.

Last but not least, my thanks to Ralph Teevan. If you hadn't received an induction order long ago, I probably would never have become a draft counselor, a lawyer, or the author of this book. It's all your fault.

ISBN   0-87337-006-6
©1985 R. Charles Johnson

READ ALL ABOUT IT!

• NOLO UPDATE SERVICE •

The material in this book is up to date at the time of printing, but the rules and regulations can change, and from time to time they do. For this reason, you should make sure you have the most recent edition of this book. But why take chances? If you mail us the coupon below, together with a **stamped, self-addressed envelope**, we will notify you if any important changes take place in the next year.

HANDY COUPON

Nolo Press, 4022 Harrison Grade, Sebastopol, CA 95472

Dear Nolo: Please notify me if there are any changes that I'll need to know about. Gee, thanks.

Name_____

Address_____

_____ Zip _____

PART ONE: THE OPENING GAME
****** REGISTRATION ******

PART TWO: THE MIDDLE GAME
**** CLASSIFICATION *****

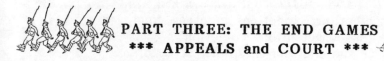

PART THREE: THE END GAMES
*** APPEALS and COURT ***

APPENDIXES

PART ONE:
THE OPENING GAME

REGISTRATION

A HEADNOTE ABOUT FOOTNOTES

Footnotes have a tendency to drive me crazy. I mean, there you are trying to read something and every few sentences there is a little number urging you to the back of the book to see what it says. In the process you lose your place and forget what the main text was saying. Well, this book has a different idea:

Do Not Read The Footnotes[*]

I'm serious about this. The footnotes in this book are only references to the law. You don't need to read them at all unless you want to know exactly what regulation or court case backs up the point being made in the book. If you just want to know the law without specific references, you can ignore the footnotes entirely.

---

[*] I told you not to read this!

FOREWORD!

This book contains the highlights of information and advice that I developed in over fifteen years of draft counseling and lawyering. This book is not a substitute for good draft counseling. Rather, the purpose is to give you enough information about the draft and your alternatives to allow you to make intelligent decisions. With good information you can get a lot more help from your draft counselor, since you can get down to real business instead of spending a lot of time discussing basic things.

How to protect yourself

When dealing with Selective Service it is important to realize that the system is not set up to protect your rights. In most cases your rights will be glossed over or denied unless you observe the rules closely and insist upon everything you are entitled to. By following the suggestions listed here you can help to insure that none of your rights gets trampled upon.

1. **Keep a file** that contains everything Selective Service sends you, and a copy of everything you send to them.

2. **Communicate in writing** with Selective Service, whether it concerns registration, change of address, a request for deferment or exemption, an appeal, or anything else.

3. Use certified mail, return receipt requested, whenever mailing anything to Selective Service.

4. Keep Selective Service informed of your address. Not only is it the law that you must do so, but it is **essential** that mail reach you in time for you to exercise your rights.

5. Meet deadlines. In most instances you will have only ten or fifteen days or less to make your move. If you don't act within the deadline, you will have lost valuable rights at that point.

6. Be prepared. The system is set up to draft people on very short notice. Men who know ahead of time what they intend to do will stand a much higher chance of success.

7. Do not rely on oral statements from Selective Service personnel. Often office clerks or board members do not know the rules, and in any case an oral statement is difficult or impossible to prove later on. If you must deal with the system by phone, get the name of the person you speak with and write a letter to SS confirming what you were told on the phone.

8. When in doubt, submit a claim. If you think you might posssibly qualify for any of the postponements, deferments, or exemptions discussed in this book, you have nothing to lose and possibly a great deal to gain by filing a claim.

9. Get help from a draft counselor. Draft counselors can look over things you receive from Selective Service, check things you intend to send them, and keep you informed of latest changes in the law or regulations that might affect you.

Draft counselors and lawyers

There are many misconceptions about draft counseling. Some people feel that draft counselors can keep men from being drafted, while others may feel that counseling is useless. Many feel that it is every man's duty to "serve his country," and that draft counselors encourage people to be unpatriotic or to break the law. Still others feel that draft counselors can give out draft deferments or exemptions.

The purpose of draft counseling is to inform people of their rights and obligations under the draft law, and to help people to make decisions that are right for them. Once you have made your decision, a counselor can help you deal with the bureaucracy of the Selective Service System. A lot of people seem to think that draft counselors can hand them a list of "ways to get out." Not only would that be impossible to do, it would also completely defeat the purpose of counseling. It is not a counselor's job to make decisions for other people, or to map out their lives for them. The purpose of counseling is to advise people of the probable consequences of their intended actions, and to help them find a course of action which will best serve their individual needs.

Each of us is an individual human being, and has the right to make his own decisions and to control his own life. No one has the right to make another person's decisions for him. Of course, there are many people who claim to have that right, such as schools, parents, friends, governments, and so on. But we are all free to decide for ourselves, and **must** decide for ourselves if we are to keep that freedom. For a draft counselor to be added to the list of people willing to control other peoples' lives would be a gross mistake.

A good counselor will make sure you are aware of all possible alternatives and probable consequences. He or she will try to learn everything possible about your personal feelings, politics and philosophy, and help you decide for yourself what you want to do. The two of you will work together toward goals **you** choose. A counselor should encourage you to take responsibility for your own life.

You **must** decide as early as possible what you want to do about the draft. The longer you wait to decide, the fewer alternatives you have left. If you don't ever decide, it may suddenly be too late. Then the government will decide for you . . . their way.

Will you go into the military if ordered? Are you going to work within the system for a deferment or exemption? Are you going to refuse to cooperate with the system? If so, at what point? Will you refuse to register for the draft? Will you refuse induction if ordered? Are you willing to go to jail or leave the country rather than cooperate with the system? These are difficult decisions to make, but a good counselor can tell you what you can expect in each case, as well as help you decide what will best serve your needs and desires, both now and in the future.

If a you already know what you want to do (perhaps as a result of reading this book) a counselor can be even more help. A counselor can help you go after the deferment or exemption you want with greatly improved chances of getting it, or set up your draft resistance case with the least chance of ending up in prison. If you want to leave the country, a counselor may be able to help you do so legally, and in a way that may permit you to come back to the United States later without facing a trial.

These things and more can be done, but it takes a lot of will-power, knowledge, and just plain hard work. Don't expect it to be easy, because it isn't. But then again, going into the military is no picnic, either.

Most big cities have draft counseling centers, and larger cities may have more than one. These centers are usually staffed by non-lawyer draft counselors, although many centers have lawyers who volunteer time as well. With a few exceptions, draft counseling is a free service. Naturally, most counseling centers could put a donation to very good use. Funding for draft counseling is usually difficult to get, and even a dollar or two would be a big help in paying office rent or phone bills.

In addition to these "lay counselors," there are also lawyers who specialize in draft law cases. Draft law is not learned in law school, so being a lawyer, even a good criminal defense lawyer, does not indicate an ability to handle draft cases. Many of the tactics which lawyers use in handling other administrative agency cases, or criminal defense cases, simply will not work in a draft case. By the same token, many of the most useful tactics and defenses in draft cases exist nowhere else in the law. The Selective Service System is a bureaucracy with its own extensive set of rules and regulations. The area of draft law is highly specialized, and only someone intimately familiar with its intricacies is going to be able to adequately handle a draft case. Naturally, a private lawyer who handles draft cases is unlikely to take cases for free.

Dealing with the draft occurs on two levels: administrative and judicial. The administrative end involves dealing with the bureaucracy of the system--registration, applying for deferments or exemptions, and so on. For those functions either a lay counselor or a lawyer can be helpful. The judicial level involves court actions, such as

13

prosecution for violating the draft law, suing the system, and so on, and in such cases, a lawyer is needed.

Whether to work with a counselor or a lawyer must be an individual decision. Some draft counselors are highly skilled and extremely knowledgeable, while others aren't. Some will be sensitive to your needs, while others may seem to use people for their own ends. By the same token, some lawyers have vast experience in draft law, while others know less than many draft counselors. The important thing is to get the best counseling available, and to find someone you can trust and feel confident working with. Whether that means a counselor or a lawyer depends on you and your circumstances.

How to spot good counseling

There are several points to watch for in looking for a counselor. Before offering advice, a good counselor will ask many questions, either in the form of a printed questionnaire, or through discussion, or both. He will try to find out what you want to do and why. He will make sure that you are fully aware of all the alternatives open to you, and will be willing to discuss those choices and their probable consequences. He will ask about your beliefs and values and try to understand them without imposing his own. Beware of a counselor who tells people "how to get out" or who "guarantees" results. He may be a knowledgeable counselor, but he also may be more interested in his own point of view than in yours. And, after all, it is **your** life and **your** decisions that are being discussed.

By the way, "he" may be "she," as some of the best counselors are women, but it seemed awkward to keep saying "he or she" over and over again.

No draft counselor or lawyer knows the answer to every question. A good counselor never guesses. If he

14

doesn't know the answer to a question, he will say so. If the information is important to you, the counselor will know where to find the answer, and will help you find it.

Since people and the law are constantly changing, the information a counselor gives one man may not be valid for others, and may not even be valid for anyone several months later. A good counselor will encourage you to stay in touch. Counseling is rarely a one-shot affair. It may take weeks, months or even years for a person to make decisions and act on them. A counselor will offer moral support through the rough times, as well as help you re-evaluate your position whenever you feel the need.

The way to spot a good draft lawyer is basically the same as looking for a good counselor. As with counselors, be wary of any lawyer who "guarantees" that he can keep you from being drafted. No one can guarantee any such thing, and anyone who claims to be able to do so is not being truthful. Even in seemingly clear-cut cases, things can go wrong and the individual can end up being drafted.

Another common area for caution is the lawyer who boasts of his "win record" being 100%, or some other high figure. While it may seem impressive at first, it might only mean that this lawyer refuses to take any difficult cases. As a fellow lawyer, I have more respect for a lawyer with a lower "win record" who takes really tough cases and still manages to pull some off. Best of all, I prefer a lawyer who doesn't bother to keep track of percentages.

People who decide to work with a lawyer are going to have to be prepared to pay legal fees. Fees vary from place to place, and from lawyer to lawyer. Some lawyers charge a flat fee, while others charge an hourly rate. A few phone calls in your community should give you a good idea of what the "average" legal fees are like.

One last word of caution--you are better off finding one counselor or lawyer you feel comfortable with and sticking with that person. One of the easiest ways I know of for you to screw up your case is to take bits and pieces of advice from several counselors. We all work a little differently, and shopping around for the easiest answers may be the kiss of death.

If you need help finding a draft counselor or lawyer near you, get in touch with one of the organizations listed in the back of this book, and they will help you. A national list grows and changes too frequently to be printed here, as it would almost immediately become outdated. However, the organizations listed in Appendix B are permanent and in touch with draft counseling across the nation.

HOW THE DRAFT SYSTEM WORKS

It is important to understand how the system works in order to anticipate what it will do to you, and to be able to get what you want from it. As my grandfather used to tell me, "The more you know about the rules of a game, the luckier you are at it."

The Selective Service System as it existed during the Vietnam era was a cumbersome, bumbling bureaucracy. Draft registrants who knew how the system operated were often able to hog-tie it in its own red tape and avoid being drafted. The system designed for use in the eighties has been streamlined in many respects, but it still has a number of vague or contradictory provisions.

The Selective Service System exists because of the Military Selective Service Act[1]—the draft law. That law has been on the books continuously since 1948 and is in effect right now. It authorizes the Selective Service System to exist, and authorizes the President to order draft registration, when and as he pleases, of men between the ages of eighteen and twenty-six. He also has the authority **right now** to classify those men, order them for physical examinations, and do everything except actually order them to be inducted into the military. The Congressional debate during the summer of 1980 was **not** over the President's authority to register men. He already had that authority. It was only over the budget appropriation to pay for draft registration.

At present, only men born in 1960 and later years are required to register. No one is currently being classified, ordered for a physical examination, or otherwise processed, but the possibility of those steps occurring is very real. Under the streamlined draft system, it could all begin very swiftly and without much warning.

The System exists on three levels: local, regional and national. At present, the national level is made up of a handful of government employees (many of them military reserve officers) who write regulations, answer questions from the government and the public, maintain the computers that hold information about men who have been registered for the draft, and generally run the show.

There are six regional Selective Service offices, each covering several states. Each regional office is headed by a military officer. Those officers are in charge of planning for facilities and personnel in the event of a draft, selecting and training volunteers to serve on local and appellate claims boards, and general support activities. Each state also has a State Director whose job is to oversee Selective Service operations within his state.

The System exists at the local level in two forms: area offices and claim boards. There are numerous area offices, each overseeing and supporting the operations of several local claims boards. In the event of a draft, the area offices will also decide all claims for administrative classifications.[2] (See Chapter 5.)

Claims boards -- more commonly called local boards -- are groups of five local residents who volunteer to serve on the board without pay.[3] Each local board covers a certain geographical area. Some counties have only one local board, while some large cities may have dozens of local boards.[4] To serve on a local board a person must be between the ages of eighteen and sixty-five, must live in the area which the board covers, and must be recommended by the Governor of the state and approved by the President of the United States.[5]

The local boards will decide claims for judgmental classifications (see Chapter 6) and will also decide appeals in cases where the area office has denied certain administrative claims.[6]

In most cases a claim denied by a local board can be appealed to a District Appeal Board. There is one District Appeal Board for each federal court district.[7] Like local board members, the District Appeal Board members are people living within that area who volunteer to serve without pay.[8]

It is important to remember that the entire system is in place and ready to go. Selective Service now has hundreds of paid employees and military reservists ready to staff the national, regional, and area offices. More than ten thousand volunteers have been appointed and trained for their jobs as members of local and appeal boards. All rules, regulations, forms and procedures needed to begin drafting have been completed and are in place. Selective Service has conducted several "dry run" exercises to test its ability to begin drafting at a moment's notice.

Outside the Selective Service System, but working hand-in-glove with it, are the military-run Military Entrance Processing Stations (MEPS). These stations administer physical exams to all people entering the military, both those who enlist and those who are drafted.[9] Only the MEPS can find someone physically unfit for induction.[10] More information about physical exemptions appears in Chapter 12.

For inductions to begin, Congress would first have to pass a bill authorizing inductions (and presumably

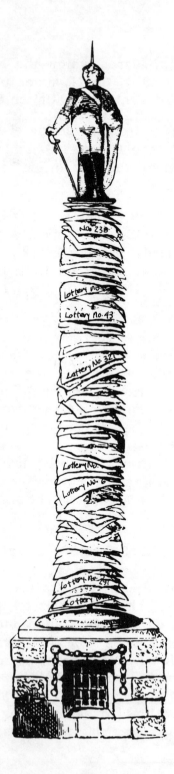

appropriating funds as well).[11] That could occur after prolonged debate, or it could happen in one day, with no warning or debate. The **same** day Congress authorizes inductions, lottery drawings will be held to determine the order in which men will be drafted. (See Chapter 4.) That **same day**, those receiving low lottery numbers will automatically be sent orders to report for induction as soon as ten days later.

Claims for deferment or exemption from the draft will have to be made within that ten day period or forever given up.[12]

As soon as induction orders begin going out, local boards and area offices will be activated to hear deferment or exemption claims. Physical examinations at MEPS will be given, perhaps on a massive scale of up to 7,000 per day, six days per week. The exams will be given on the day you report for induction. If you are found physically qualified and have not requested a deferment or exemption, you will be inducted into the military that day.

Your classification will determine whether or not you will be inducted. The Selective Service System uses eighteen classifications to categorize men subject to the draft. If you are classified into some of those categories, your induction will be postponed. This is called a "deferment." If you fall into certain of the other categories, you will not be subject to the draft at all. This is called "exemption."

At the beginning you will be presumed to be 1-A, eligible for draft. But if you act fast you can apply for reclassification to another category which will defer or exempt you from induction. Part Two of this book explains how to understand and use the rules on classification to your best advantage.

The urgent need to be prepared

When induction notices first go out, claims for deferment or exemption will have to be made within 10 days of the date the notices were mailed or forever given up.[13]

Anyone wishing to obtain a draft deferment or exemption cannot afford to delay. With only days in which to request deferment or exemption, it is absolutely essential that claims be prepared well ahead of time. Once inductions begin, draft counselors will be swamped and unable to give individual attention to very many men, if any. Civilian doctors willing to document existing grounds for medical exemption will be able to see only a very few of those needing their services. The release of medical records alone could take far longer than ten days. The documentation needed for other deferment or exemption claims may not be available on such short notice. If you wait until it hits the fan, it may be too late to duck.

During Vietnam most people ordered for induction were put into the Army, but thousands ended up in the Marine Corps. In either event, most draftees ended up in combat units on the front lines in Vietnam. Is that something you are willing to do? If you don't make your decision, the government will make it for you.

There are many alternatives available to you and many ways you can deal with the draft. These are all discussed in the following pages, but the success of most plans depends upon getting an early start on your preparation and planning. It is never too late to start planning, but it is never too early, either. An early start on a good plan gives you an excellent chance of getting your way with the system. That's what the rest of this book is about.

ENLISTING TO BEAT THE DRAFT

People sometimes consider the possibility of enlisting in the military as an alternative to being drafted. If you want to join the military, that is your business. But before you do so, give some thought to this Chapter. If you don't want to go into the military, then enlisting in order to keep from being drafted makes about as much sense as destroying a village in order to save it (a bit of double-think that was popular during the Vietnam war).

Some men enlist, thinking they can get a better deal than if they are drafted. This is what recruiters would like you to think, but it is not necessarily true. If you do decide to enlist in the military the local recruiters will no doubt be very happy to help you, but before you do it a few words of caution are in order.

Reserves, National Guard & Coast Guard

During the Vietnam war it became common for people to enlist in a branch of the military reserves to avoid being drafted and sent to Vietnam. While it worked then, people considering the reserves today should give it some deep thought. When the United States became involved in Southeast Asia in the mid-sixties, the military wanted to send thousands of troops overseas immediately. Draft calls shot up, but draftees take several months to train. In order to quickly meet the rising demand for trained personnel, tens of thousands of military reservists were called to active duty and many were sent to Vietnam. It was only later in the war that active duty strength was high enough to meet military manpower requirements, and the reserves became known as an outfit of weekend soldiers.

If the United States becomes involved in another war there is every reason to believe that a similar pattern will occur, and that reservists will be called to active duty in large numbers early in the war. If you join a reserve unit now you may only be insuring that you will be sent into battle if another war occurs in the next several years.

Even if there is no war in the immediate future, enlistment in the reserves is a major commitment. Most reservists are required to enlist for a period of at least eight years. Anywhere from six months to two years of that time is spent on active duty. The remainder is spent attending "reserve meetings" one weekend each month, plus a full two weeks on active duty each year. Many reservists find such a schedule to be extremely stressful. They are civilians most of the time, but are required to play soldier or sailor during one full weekend each month in addition to spending their two week "vacation" on active duty each year.

A reservist who misses weekend reserve meetings can be punished by being placed on active duty for twenty-four months (less any active duty time already served) or for forty-five days (if he has already served two years or more on active duty). A reservist who does not report for the two-week activation each year can be court-martialed for being AWOL.

Another possibility some people consider is the National Guard. You should consider that Guard members, like reservists, are members of the military: Army National Guard members are in the Army, and Air National Guard members are in the Air Force. They are subject to a period of active duty (usually six months) and, like other reservists, are required to attend monthly meetings and annual activations under threat of permanent active duty assignment for missed meetings or courts-martial for missing activations.

While I don't recall any Guard members being sent to Vietnam, they could be called into any battle since they are military reservists. In any event, many Guard members have found themselves activated to "control" anti-war and civil rights demonstrations at home. Could you aim a loaded gun at someone you work or go to school with, and fire if ordered? Many Guardsmen were ordered to do just that not so long ago.

What about the Coast Guard? Some people seem to feel that the Coast Guard is not a military organization, but look: they wear military uniforms, have military rank, hold military inspections, and are subject to military law, rules and regulations. In other words, the Coast Guard is a military organization. In the past several years the Coast Guard's biggest job has been making pot busts, but during the Vietnam war many of the Vietnamese rivers and deltas were regularly patrolled by Coast Guard cutters.

Enlistment promises and contracts

Military recruiters all have one thing in common: they are anxious to fill their quotas. As a result, many thousands of people have been enlisted illegally, and tens of thousands more have been enlisted legally but found that they weren't going to get what was promised to them by the recruiter. Military recruiters will often promise almost anything, but unless the promises appear in writing on the enlistment contract they are generally worthless. The usual principles of contract law often do not apply to military enlistment contracts, and even when they do apply the courts are prone to interpreting the contracts in favor of the military, not the individual soldier or sailor.

Promises that you will receive a particular kind of job training may be a joke. For instance, if you enlist to go to electronics school you may find yourself pulling wires instead of learning electronics. Recruiters have been known to enlist people for schools for which they are not qualified—being dropped from a military training school for academic reasons does not void out your enlistment contract. You will be stuck for the rest of the enlistment period, and you can be assigned to whatever job the military wants to give you.

Even if you complete the training there is no guarantee that you will be allowed to work in your field—they may decide to assign you as a cook, supply sergeant, or even an infantryman on the front lines. Many of the "skills" taught in military schools have no civilian counter-part: how many classified ads have you seen lately looking for trained tank mechanics or missile guidance system repairmen?

Guaranteed duty stations can also be a rip-off. Many men enlisted in the Army during Vietnam because they were promised they would be stationed in Germany or Hawaii, and that sounded better than Vietnam. Sure enough, they were sent to Germany or Hawaii . . . for ten months. Their next tour of duty was in lovely Southeast Asia where they could bask in the fragrant warmth of napalm fires.

The bottom line is that the military gives no guarantees that are permanent, and few that are even reliable. All members are expected to serve on the front lines at any time, any job or place of duty can be changed whenever "military convenience" dictates, reservists can be activated and active duty contracts can be involuntarily extended in times of "military mobilization," and enlistment contracts can be broken by the military almost at will.

Tips for enlistees

If you are thinking of enlisting in the military, you would be well advised to protect yourself and keep the recruiters honest. Whenever you discuss things with a recruiter, have a witness with you. Get all promises in writing on the enlistment contract and initialed by the recruiter. Thoroughly read everything before you sign it. If there is anything you don't understand, take it to a civilian counselor or lawyer trained in military law. Don't believe the recruiter's explanation of what it means until you check it out with someone who isn't biased.

Find out what day-to-day life is like in the branch you are interested in by talking with other people (not recruiters) who are currently on active duty or have recently been in. If possible, talk with someone who has taken the school you are considering, or served in the location you have been promised, to see if your expectations are too high. A free trip to Europe at Army expense sounds wonderful but the realities of Army life in Europe can be grim.

Most importantly, explore your own needs and desires. Are you really ready to sign away two, three, four or more years of your life? Is the military the best thing for you to do right now? Will you still be willing to remain on active duty or in the reserves if a war starts up?

Far too many people enlist on the spur of the moment, and for poor reasons such as broken love affairs, fights with parents, or loss of a job. Those experiences last only a short while, but an enlistment contract lasts a long, long time. Think carefully before signing one. It is easy to enlist, but very difficult to change your mind once you are in.

REGISTRATION AND RESISTANCE

The law says that all male US citizens and most resident aliens (non-US citizens) between the ages of eighteen and twenty-six can be required to register as the President may direct.[1] Currently the government has called for the registration of men born in 1960 and later years. At present, you are required to register within thirty days of your eighteenth birthday.[2] The maximum penalty for violating the draft law, such as by not registering on time, is up to five years in prison and/or a ten thousand dollar fine.[3]

The registration is done by use of forms available at Post Offices throughout the country, and at US Embassy offices in foreign countries. If you don't register when required to do so, you have broken the law. The only exception is if you can show good reasons for not having registered, such as if you were hospitalized at the time.

While there are many people who think they will immediately be thrown into prison if they are caught for non-registration, the truth is that most people who have not registered in the past have never seen the inside of a courthouse, let alone a prison. This fear of prison is the image that Selective Service likes people to have. There is nothing that motivates people like fear, and that is one of the reasons people call Selective Service "the SS."

As of 1984, somewhere between ten and twelve million men have registered with the SS. Somewhere between 500,000 and 1,500,000 have declined to register, depending upon whose figures you want to believe. Of all the nonregistrants, fewer than two dozen have had charges brought against them. The published word has a way of tarnishing, so by the time you read this it may be that hundreds of non-registrants will have been prosecuted. But maybe not. So far, the government's track record for prosecution is far from intimidating.

Non-registration is breaking the law, and I certainly don't mean to encourage anyone to break the law. After all, that's illegal! But just for fun let's look at what it means to "break the law."

Laws are rules--guidelines for social conduct. Supposedly they reflect the ideal of the society, although sometimes they don't actually do so. It is doubtful whether many people really care whether they break a law or not. At one time or another almost everyone has run a stop sign, driven too fast, jay-walked, or somehow broken the law. What most people care about is whether or not they get caught breaking the law, and if caught what their penalty will be.

Some people have pointed to statistics from the Vietnam draft which show that only about ten percent of the men who violated the draft law were actually prosecuted, but those figures are misleading. The vast majority of those cases involved men who refused to be inducted. Under the system then being used, it took months or years of processing by the system before an induction order could be issued. If a man could show that his induction order resulted from improper processing (which was often the case) he would not be prosecuted for refusing induction, but would be sent back to the local board for further processing. In many other cases a man who had refused induction would find that he had no legal defense to the charges. Rather than face conviction and a possible prison sentence, thousands of men agreed to accept induction if re-ordered, or to enlist in the military in order to avoid prosecution.

In other words, while nine out of ten cases may not have been prosecuted, very few draft law violators actually succeeded in avoiding the draft and avoiding prosecution.

The potential non-registrant should also consider that the Vietnam statistics are largely based on the charge of refusing induction. While no statistics are immediately available, most draft counselors and draft lawyers from that era agree that men who refused to register usually stood a much higher chance of being tried, convicted, and sentenced to prison than did those who registered on time but later chose to refuse induction. Again, this was due to the increased possibility of erroneous processing by Selective Service, which would give rise to a defense.

Finally, for those who think that nonregistration is attractive because, say, only one out of a thousand nonregistrants ends up in prison: how comforting are those odd if _you_ are the one in a thousand? Will you feel better knowing that 999 others got away with it?

In favor of nonregistration

A case in favor of not registering for the draft was made by David Wayte, one of the first of the few men to be prosecuted for non-registration in the 1980s. The following is in his own words:

"Whether one be a religious, ethical, or political objector, the decision not to register is always an intensely personal one. For this reason, the non-registrant needs both support for his stand and respect for his values and beliefs. It is an immense benefit to know that someone is there who not only agrees with your beliefs, but supports you as a person.

"Not registering for the draft was never an easy decision for me. Hanging over my head was the vague but ever-present threat of a prison term, with all the fears and uncertainties that go with it. Besides that was the nagging and seductive doubt that, well, it's only registration, and maybe I'm making a lot of trouble over nothing.

"There were always political considerations. The fact that draft registration is a vital facet of a vast military build-up. The fact that it could only be used to fight intervention-type wars in Third World countries. The fact that it was meant to create a psychological atmosphere whereby young people would respond to the call to war without questions or reservations.

"Then there was my own moral and ethical viewpoint. I knew that draft registration was a cog in the machinery of war. I knew that by registering I would be contributing to my government's preparation for war. I would make myself available, a blank check for my government to use as it wished. For me, to register would be to surrender responsibility for my own actions. I would become less of a person. War is only organized murder, and I did not want to kill, nor did I want to lend my support to such a system.

"In the end, my reasons were instinctive. I simply could not visualize my name on the registration card. There was something inside me which wouldn't let me do it. Whatever the consequences, draft registration was not for me.

"At first I was quite confident that I would be prosecuted, and in fact welcomed the idea. Later on, as the fanfare died down, and as I heard numerous stories about the horrors of prison life, I developed a certain dread of what was to come. My greatest fear was of being caught alone in the system, unrecognized, having stuck my neck out for a cause which was soon to pass.

"When I finally received by first warning letters from the system, I was amazed at how placating the government was. I had ample opportunity to register whenever I wanted to. The government would much rather that I recant my position and register, than for it to go through the trouble and risk of bringing me to trial.

"I think that this is an important point for a young man facing registration to remember. The government will go to almost any length to avoid prosecuting you. You can always register late, and Selective Service will be more than happy to receive your name. If you decide not to register, you can always change your mind later, but if you do register, you can never take that back.

"If you decide not to register, you won't be alone. That is a simple fact.

"When I decided not to register, I knew I had to go public. In the first place, I'm terrible at keeping a secret, and I'm very susceptible to paranoia. But most of all, I wanted to take as strong a stand as possible, and going public allowed me to reach out to the greatest number of people. It was also the most honest and straight-forward thing to do. I also felt that if enough of us refuse to register, there is no way they can put us all in prison."

Leave the country?

People outside the country who do not register when required to do so are in violation of the draft law, the same as if they were inside the US. It is extremely unlikely that the FBI would bother to track down anyone outside the country who hasn't registered, and a person cannot usually be extradited to the United States for non-registration. However, anyone required to register who has not done so may run into troubles if he ever returns to US soil--which includes US embassies in other countries.

People who leave the United States after having registered will continue to be processed. Again, it is unlikely that a person would be extradited to the US for failure to comply with an induction order or other SS order, but if he ever returned to the US he would most likely be arrested and prosecuted. The same applies to anyone who refuses to register while in the US and later leaves the country.

However, a person who is not a United States citizen or resident alien at the time he would be required to register for the draft need not register. For instance, if a person left the United States at age seventeen and became (or already was) a citizen of some other country, he would not be required to register for the draft unless he later became a permanent resident alien, an illegal alien, or a United States citizen. It is possible that a person in this situation could return to the US at some later time, but such a tactic could result in his being denied US citizenship, and could even bar him from ever re-entering the US, even as a visitor. People considering this option should discuss it thoroughly with a lawyer who understands both draft law and immigration law.

Non-citizens who are currently living in the US, and dual nationals (citizens of both the US and some other country) are covered by several special provisions of the draft law. For more on that subject, see Appendix A.

For the majority of draft-age men, leaving the country is no real solution. It is also not that easy. During the Vietnam war some foreign countries welcomed men who were evading the draft—two of the best known being Canada and Sweden. The catch is that those policies were political statements of disapproval of US involvement in Vietnam. When the Vietnam war ended, so did the Canadian and Swedish policies favoring US draft evaders. When draft registration resumed in 1980, both Sweden and Canada publicly announced that US draft evaders would receive no special treatment, but would be treated the same as all other foreigners seeking entry. It is no longer possible to receive official permission to live in those countries without going through regular channels, including an application submitted before entry.

In other words, while it is a cinch to cross the border into, say, Canada, if you overstay your visit you will be an illegal alien subject to deportation back to the US. If you are wanted on a draft charge, the odds are good that the FBI will be waiting to welcome you home. Even if you manage to evade detection by Canadian officials, your illegal status would make life difficult. You will not be eligible for an employment permit or for any human services such as unemployment benefits, public a-ssistance, and perhaps medical attention.

Non-registration?

If you decide not to register when required, there are some things that can better your odds of avoiding trial if caught, and also better your chances of avoiding prison if tried and convicted. The first question at hand, though, is what do you hope to accomplish by not registering? There are, of course, as many reasons for

35

not registering as there are non-registrants. Since motives are sometime an important issue in court trials, no one should decide not to register without first deciding why he is refusing to register.

One point of view is that non-registration is a political statement: a man feels that the draft law is wrong, should not be allowed to exist, and therefore refuses to comply with it in any way. People who take this stand often make public announcements of their non-registration and use every opportunity they can find to publicly denounce the draft. Of course, if you make your position public it is almost certain that the SS will eventually catch up with you, but that doesn't automatically mean you will end up in jail. In the past, most non-registrants have been given at least one "warning," a notice that the SS had no record of their registration, and advising them to register immediately. If they decided at that time to register, they would usually just get put in with the other registrants. However, men who register late can still be prosecuted at some later time. Late registration may stall off **immediate** prosecution, but it does not erase the violation from your records.

On the other hand, if your conscience will not allow you to register, there is a possibility you will be taken to court, and perhaps sent to prison. I don't encourage people to go to prison. To the contrary, with so many options for avoiding the draft legally, I encourage people to comply with the law as far as their conscience will allow. However, one must respect those committed people who intelligently make the decision to take prison instead of the draft.

Another way to look at non-registration is to regard it as a more personal action. People who refuse to register for personal reasons may not be as concerned with political action as with their own situation or their own conscience, or they may feel that a political movement can be strong without being vocal. Those are perfectly respectable points of view.

Non-registration is not an easy way out

No one should fail to register because he thinks it is the "easy way out." There are many legal ways to avoid being drafted, but non-registration is not one of them. If you refuse to register, you are breaking the law, and that is not a game—it is a rugged way of life. Any refusal to cooperate with the SS, including non-registration, is known as resistance. You are taking a stand against the law, and you may go through hell for it.

Resistance is not a choice for people looking for an easy way out. It is a difficult road to travel, and a man taking it will probably have his life affected for years, perhaps forever. He stands a chance of ending up in prison for up to five years,[4] especially if he decides not to register even after being warned. War resisters don't come out of jail as heroes; they come out as convicted felons.

People convicted of draft law violations lose many of their civil rights in most states. It is a felony, meaning that in many states they lose their right to vote, and may not be allowed to practice law or medicine. Some states, such as California, do not penalize draft law violators so harshly, since they look to see if a man's felony conviction involved "moral turpitude." But most states, and many major employers, are prejudiced against all felons.

Federal pens are no picnic, either. You will come into contact with some really hardened people . . . perverts, addicts, sadists, fascists, murderers, and so on. And those are just the guards--some of the prisoners are pretty bad, too.

Resistance is definitely not for the weak-at-heart, or for people who aren't sure what they want to do about the draft. Deciding to resist is a very real commitment. It is a decision that should be thought over very carefully. It is probably the biggest and most difficult decision a draft-age man has ever had to make. You should be sure you know what you are getting into before committing yourself to it, and should talk it over with someone you trust before making a final decision.

Going underground?

Many people feel very dedicated to non-registration, but don't feel that they want to make their resistance public. Getting out of the draft by not registering can work, but it can also get you a difficult future. It may mean the possibility of prosecution hanging over you for years to come. To avoid punishment, a person would have to avoid being detected for many years. Just how many years is not completely clear. The general statute of limitations says that federal felonies cannot be charged if more than five years have elapsed since the offense was committed.[5] However, in 1971 Congress added a provision to the Selective Service Act which says that nonregistrants can be charged until they reach age thirty-one.[6] The other catch is that the statute of limitations does not apply if you have been underground, outside the country, or otherwise unavailable for prosecution,[7] nor does it apply in cases where charges have been filed, even if the charges have never been served.[8]

If you were to decide not to register, and also not to make your act a public statement, and assuming you wanted to avoid getting caught for as long as possible, then you may want to know how others in your situation have handled the problem. Once again, I want to make it clear that I do not advise anyone to break the law.

Some people, while not being overtly public, are still so proud of their non-registration that they let on (brag) to people they know that they haven't registered. This is fine if you want to take a public stand, but it is a damned poor way to keep a secret. Sooner or later the wrong person is going to hear about it and "patriotically" turn you in. Or someone will have a grievance with you and "get even" by turning you in. Ironically, the majority of non-registrants who do get caught are turned in by family members or ex-lovers.

Other non-registrants seem to become paranoid. They turn pale if anyone mentions the draft. They run and hide if they see a policeman. They change jobs often and are constantly on the move, even though no one is actually after them. They are always looking over their shoulders, and don't trust people. They become loners. Their behavior is often so suspicious that people become suspicious of them, fulfilling their own fears, sometimes causing them to eventually get caught.

One of the more common ways for non-registrants to be caught is by being arrested for some other charge. Even being stopped for running a stop sign or having a faulty automobile tail light could result in a police check on your name. If the computer bank shows that you may be a non-registrant, you will suddenly have problems far more serious than running a stop sign.

Another possible catch for non-registrants comes from schools. Some high schools and colleges perform a "public service" by sending the SS and military recruiters a list of students. If you received a rash of recruiting literature at about the time you graduated from high school, there is a good chance that the system knows you exist. This means it will be easy for them to track you down. Consequently, you may find yourself moving around a lot, and developing all the paranoid tendencies described above. It's no fun!

Within the past few years the government has come up with a few other programs for tracking down nonregistrants. These programs involve comparing the names in the SS computer with the names in other government computers, such as Social Security, Internal Revenue, and state driver's license records. If your name is listed in any such data banks, the odds are overwhelming that the SS will track you down.

Another attack on nonregistrants has been championed by Congressman Gerald Solomon (R-NY) who has succeeded in getting laws passed which require draft-age men who apply for various programs and benefits to certify that they have registered. At this time there are two such laws: one applies to student financial aid applicants and the other to benefits under the Job Training Partnership Act. Legal challenges have resulted in a US Supreme Court opinion upholding the student aid law.

If caught

As mentioned above, most people caught in the past for non-registration have been given a choice: register or face trial. If a person decides to register at that point he won't automatically be drafted--he will be put in with the rest of the registrants and treated exactly the same as everyone else. Of course, someone may want to know why he didn't register on time. It may be that, as a matter of conscience, he didn't feel that he could be a part of the war machine, but has now decided that his registering won't necessarily mean being a part of it. If so, he may be qualified for a conscientious objector classification, and want to explain that in writing.

In any event, the system wants people to register. The SS is likely to accept just about any reason given for late registration. Some lawyers, including myself, contend that a person doesn't have to provide a statement explaining his late registration. By simply supplying the system with what it needs to register you, you are fulfilling your legal obligation. People who decide to give a reason should realize that even though they are being allowed to register late, they can still be prosecuted for late registration up to five years later.[9] Any statement they make concerning their late registration could later be used as evidence against them.

A number of nonregistrants have registered as much as a year or two late, some after receiving warning letters from the SS or the US attorney, or because the FBI had come looking for them, or because it was the only way to receive financial aid for their educations. Others made the decision when they realized the chance of ever being prosecuted for late registration is small, and for various reasons they found that their chance for being drafted was also small.

Some men have misunderstood what it means to register. Registering for the draft does not mean that you will ever be called—that depends on the draft mechanism discussed in the next chapter, and most of all on whether the draft is being used. The fact is that no one has been drafted in this country for over ten years. That is, of course, no guarantee that the draft won't be fired up next week.

The handful of nonregistrants who have been prosecuted during the last few years have not fared all that well in court. Of the eight men who have gone to trial, all have been found guilty. Five were sentenced to prison terms ranging from thirty-five days to thirty months, and three were placed on probation. One conviction was reversed on appeal; several trials are still pending. The small number of cases does not make a meaningful statistic, but it is worth knowing about.

An interesting defense was raised by Enten Eller, the first man since Vietnam to go to trial on a draft charge. He contended that his religious beliefs would not allow him to take part in war or the preparation for war, including draft registration. The judge ruled that conscientious objection (see Chapter 7) is not a valid defense to nonregistration, and found Eller guilty. Several older cases also say that nonregistration charges cannot be defended by the Freedom of Religion Clause in the First Amendment, or by the fact that if the man had registered he would have qualified as a conscientious objector or for some other deferment or exemption.[10]

Registration procedure

Registration for the draft is currently being handled by Post Offices. The actual process consists of providing the SS with enough information to allow them to locate you if they decide to draft you. A form is provided for you to fill out. It asks for your name, sex, date of birth, social security number, current phone number, and two addresses--a current mailing address and permanent residence.

The law says that you have to register within thrity days of your eighteenth birthday.[11] That actually means a sixty-one day period beginning thirty days before your birthday and lasting until thirty days afterward. The SS has announced that early registration will be accepted up to 120 days before you turn eighteen. I'm sure you'll be glad to know about that.

Some registrants have been known to provide the address of a friend or relative as their official address. That seems to be perfectly legal, since the law does not require you to let the SS know where you are living, just that you keep them informed of an address where mail will regularly and promptly be delivered to you.

Some men have provided false addresses when registering. Not only is that illegal, it could also work against you. There are many times when you can preserve your rights **only** if you respond to mail sent out by the SS within a very short time, such as ten or fifteen days from mailing. Providing a false address, or an address where mail will not reach you promptly, may mean missing deadlines and losing advantages that might have been gained.

It is important for you to understand that you are legally responsible for receiving your mail from the SS, and that the Post Office is forbidden by law from forwarding mail from them to you, even if you have filled out a change of address notice. You **must** keep the SS notified of an address where you can be sure of receiving any mail they may send.

There is no reason why the registration form must be filled out right there in the Post Office. In fact, it would seem to make a great deal of sense to take the form to a draft counselor and discuss how to answer the questions posed. That is especially true if you have a choice of addresses, or wish to pursue ultimate deferment or exemption from the draft.

Another point to bear in mind is that you don't have to appear for registration at the Post Office which covers the area where you really live. For instance, let's say that your mailing address is San Francisco, but you are currently going to school in Chicago. You could show up at any Post Office in Chicago, fill out the form, and be registered. If you give the San Francisco address on your registration form, that is where your SS mail will go.

The registration form does not contain any opportunity to claim deferment or exemption from the draft. There has been some talk of adding a box to check if you feel that you are a conscientious objector, but Congress has refused to authorize it.

Before turning a completed registration form over to a Postal clerk, you would be well advised to make at least two photocopies of the form as filled out, including any statements on the form about being qualified for a deferment or exemption. If possible, you should have a witness accompany you to the Post Office when the form is turned in. There are two reasons for making copies and having a witness:

First: Postal employees have been instructed not to give any receipts for completed registration forms. If the Post Office manages to lose it, or if the SS somehow fails to get the information properly programmed into its computer, you will have no proof that you registered. But, if you have a photocopy of the registration form, and a witness who saw you turn in the original, you will have proof. To play really safe, you can have your witness indicate on one photocopy that the witness saw you hand in the original form at a stated Post Office, and the witness can date and sign the photocopy. That copy can then be placed in an envelope and mailed to you. The envelope should not be opened or tampered with when it is delivered. If any question ever arises as to whether you registered when required to do so, the postmarked, **sealed** envelope containing the photocopy and the witness's statement can be presented to a judge. That should provide more than enough proof.

Second: Even if no trouble comes up about your having registered on time, the witnessed photocopy can serve another purpose. Once the SS computerizes the information on your registration form, the original form will be destroyed. If you claimed on the registration form that you are a conscientious objector, that information will **not** be fed into the SS computer. Once the form is destroyed, you will have no proof that you registered as a conscientious objector unless you kept a copy of the form. Further, the fact that the copy of the form is contained in a post-marked, sealed envelope dated the same day you registered provides proof that your original registration form really did indicate your conscientious objection. This way there can be no suspicion that you might have later filled out a registration form saying you are a conscientious objector.

The Post Office will send the registration form to the SS center in Great Lakes, Illinois, where the information will be fed into a computer. The only communication from the SS after registration will be a form letter sent out within ninety days after you register. The letter will acknowledge that you have registered, ask whether the information shown in the computer is correct, inform you of your legal duty to keep the SS informed of an address where mail will reach you, and assign you a Selective Service number. The SS number will be used to identify you, and should be kept, since it will be needed on all further communications with the SS, including any subsequent changes of address. If you find that the information fed into the computer is incorrect, you should notify the SS as soon as possible. And if you feel that the error in SS records is that it fails to reflect that you claimed to be a conscientious objector when you registered, you may wish to inform the SS of that fact. It probably won't force them to keep records on people who claim to be conscientious objectors, but by once again keeping a photocopy of the communication, you will start building your conscientious objector file.

In the event that more than ninety days pass after you register and you do not receive the form letter from the SS, you should immediately write a letter to them asking what has happened to your registration information. A photocopy of the letter should be kept.

Under the computerized SS process no "draft files" are set up, and there is no official opportunity to submit evidence to support a claim for any deferment or exemption until **after** an induction order has been sent to you. Only basic information will be kept, and it will all be computerized. Even so, some registrants have submitted written claims to the SS for conscientious objector status. The claims have been returned, along with a letter explaining that the SS can not accept the claim at that time.[12] Such a letter can be added to the rest of your file as further proof of your conscientious objection.

Resistance after registration

Registering does not mean that you absolutely will be drafted. It merely means that you **may** be drafted. You could get a high lottery number and not be called; you might qualify for one of several deferments or exemptions which will keep you from being drafted; or you may be able to avoid ever being called.

For many people who make the decision to register, their set of circumstances after registration brings with it the realization that they no longer care to cooperate with the system. Many of them decide to do what they can, legally or otherwise, to "jam" the system. The following discussion is not intended to encourage people to do illegal acts, but merely to report things which others have done in the past.

You have a legal duty to keep the SS informed of an address where mail will reach you.[13] That does not mean that you must report a change of address every time you move, as long as the address they have is one where mail will reach you. Even if you are working or going to school hundreds of miles from the address the SS has, you are legal so long as someone at that address will receive mail for you and send it along, or let you know when it arrives. However, if the address given to the SS is no good, or becomes no good, a failure to give them a valid address is a violation of the law punishable by up to five years in prison and/or a $10,000 fine. Mail from the SS may not legally be forwarded by the Post Office, even if you have given the Post Office a change of address form. You **must** notify the SS directly.

Some people have used address changes to jam the system. One man I know gave his parents' address when he registered, and shortly after that time he moved into an apartment a few miles away. No matter which of those addresses the SS used, mail would reach him. He realized that every time he reported a change of address, someone would have to feed new data to the computer. He just couldn't decide which address to use, and ended up changing his address every few months. Soon a number of his friends became as indecisive as he was, and it became a full time job for the SS to keep track of all their different address changes. If you want to keep the system running smoothly you are going to have to try not to change addresses as often as those fellows did.

In addition to indecisive people, the world contains many people who have poor memories. Some can't remember names, others forget birthdays and anniversaries, while others can't seem to recall even the

47

most important things . . . such as whether or not they remembered to register for the draft. These poor souls will drift through life in a fog. They will wake up in the morning and wonder aloud, "Gosh, did I register for the draft?"

There may be help for these unfortunates. A simple letter to the SS, asking whether or not they did register, will receive a response reassuring them that they did. Of course, it will take someone in the SS a little time to check the computer to see whether or not a man has registered--especially if he can't even recall his SS number. And it will take a little more time to write him a letter assuring him that all is well. But nothing is too good for our boys. And, golly, if the poor devil forgets again six months later, and again writes in to make absolutely sure that he really honestly did register for the draft, I guess the SS will just have to let him know again. And again. And again.

Whether or not to register for the draft, and once registered whether or not to resist, are not easy decisions. They should be given a great deal of thought. It may be that discussing these things with relatives, friends, ministers or draft counselors will make the decisions easier, but the final decision is yours, and yours alone. It is your life, and no one else can decide for you. As David Wayte said so well, the decision is always an intensely personal one.

PART TWO:
THE MIDDLE GAME
CLASSIFICATION

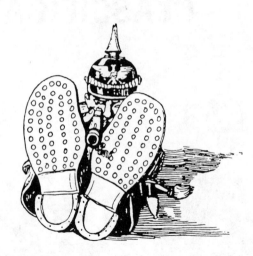

WINNING AND LOSING
IN THE DRAFT LOTTERY

The United States has a national lottery. It is only drawn occasionally, but it usually gets big media coverage when it does occur. It doesn't cost any money to participate--you just need to have been born in the right year. There are tens of thousands of potential winners, and each winner will receive a guaranteed full-time job for two years. Many winners in the past have received an all-expense-paid vacation in a foreign country, and tens of thousands of past lucky winners have even had their burial costs paid. The U.S. lottery seems somewhat warped, though, because if you win, you lose; if you lose, you win.

The draft lottery is a mechanism that is used to determine who will be drafted from among those available for selection. In actuality, lottery numbers play only a part in the draft system. The real question is: who is available for induction and who in that group is eligible? Registrants are sorted into Selection Groups by year of birth, and those groups are arranged in order of priority. The lottery is only then used to select who will be drafted from the group with the highest priority that has available registrants in it. Now let's go through it in more detail.

51

Order of call

There is an over-all system known as the "Order of Call" which affects all people who are available to be drafted. The lottery is only a part of the Order of Call, so in order to understand the lottery system you have to understand the Order of Call.

The Order of Call is a method of ranking people who are available to be drafted by putting them into various "Selection Groups" for being drafted. People in the highest group have the highest likelihood of being drafted, and will be called first whenever there is a draft call. People in the lower groups have less chance of being drafted, and will be drafted last, if ever. Here's the main point: when drafting people, the SS **must** follow the Order of Call. No one can be called from a given group until **all** people in higher groups have been called.[1]

In general terms, men are put into various selection groups according to the year in which they reach a certain age. The Age Twenty Selection Group consists of all men who will turn twenty in the current calendar year. These are men who are eligible for the first time to be drafted. At midnight on December 31, all men in that group who were not inducted will automatically rotate into the Age Twenty-One Selection Group as a fresh new crop of men enter the Age Twenty Selection Group. Happy New Year!

Like a row of dominoes, every January 1, all men who were not inducted are moved into the next selection group, so that you are always in the group named for the age you will reach in that calendar year. Selection Groups for ages twenty-six to thirty-four are only for men who were previously ordered for induction but who were not inducted because they received one of the following classifications: 1-D-D, 2-D, 3-A, 4-B, or 4-F (see Chapter 6).

No matter what lottery number you get, you can not be drafted until the calendar year during which you turn twenty. This does not mean that only twenty-year-olds can be drafted. Even if your birthday doesn't come until December 31, you could still be called up at **any** time during that year. The system is based on the calendar year of your birth, not your actual age.

The "calendar year" concept also creates another misconception. The law says that the calendar year during which you turn twenty is the **earliest** that you can be drafted.[2] However, merely getting through that year without actually being inducted into the military does not mean that you are safe. For instance, if large-scale drafting occurs it is possible that all available men could be called before the year ends. If that happens, drafting would then shift to the next oldest year-group. If that group were also used, the next oldest year-group would be called, and so on down the line until men 25 were being called.[3] It seems pretty unlikely that draft calls would be big enough to completely exhaust a year-group, but there have been calls that big in the past and it could happen again. You can't really consider yourself safe until the year in which you turn 26.

The lottery

Lottery numbers can be thought of as a more detailed order of call within the larger scheme. People who are in a particular Age Selection Group **must** be called in sequence by lottery number. It would be illegal to call people from the Age Twenty-One Selection Group without first reaching all lottery numbers in the Age Twenty Selection Group, and it would likewise be illegal to call lottery number fifty from a selection group before everyone in that group with lottery numbers one through forty-nine had first been called.

Lottery drawings are conducted separately for each different birth year. Thus, men born on the same day (say October 13) but in different years have only one chance in 365 for getting the same lottery number.

Here's how the lottery is conducted. Each day of the calendar year written down, placed in a separate plastic plastic capsule, and tossed into a bucket. Another bucket holds capsules containing the numbers 1 through 365 (or 366 if a leap year is involved). Capsules are drawn from each bucket, one at a time, and matched up, so each date of the year is assigned a number. There is no logical order to the numbers assigned. Each date of the year has an equal chance of getting lottery number 1, or number 365, or any number in between.

The dates of the year represent the birth dates of all draft registrants who were born in a given year. Everyone subject to the lottery who is born on the same date in that year gets the same lottery number. The lottery numbers themselves indicate the order in which people could be drafted: number one would be the first to go, then number two, and so on.

There is no way to change a lottery number once it has been assigned.[4] The number assigned to you is based upon the date the SS records show as your date of birth at the time the lottery drawing is held. Even if the date they have on file is wrong—if you gave the wrong date when you registered, or if someone messed up while feeding the computer—once your lottery number has been assigned you can not have it changed.

If the SS anticipates that the draft calls for the year will not reach all lottery numbers for that year-group, a "ceiling number" may be announced. For instance, in July 1972 a "ceiling number" of 100 was set for the lottery pool drawn for 1972. The ceiling number is the highest lottery number that the SS expects to draft out of that pool. There is no requirement that a ceiling number be set, and if the SS expects to draft large numbers of people it is unlikely that one will be set. For instance, if the SS intended to issue draft calls such as those issued during the Vietnam and Korean wars, it is possible that all members of the Age 20 Selection Group will be called, and therefore no ceiling number will be set.

If a ceiling number is set, anyone whose lottery number is higher than the ceiling number set for his lottery pool will most likely be classified 1-H and not be drafted, unless there is an unexpected draft increase, such as a declaration of war or national emergency. The ceiling number is **not** a guarantee that those with higher numbers won't be drafted, but once the number is set it is very unlikely that the SS will later raise it unless a national mobilization occurs. People with lottery numbers equal to or lower than the ceiling number will probably be processed for induction.

Being called does not necessarily mean being inducted. For example, let's say that a call is for all people in the Age Twenty Selection Group with lottery numbers one through fifty. A community could have twenty men in that group with those numbers, and yet not actually induct anyone. Let's say that of those twenty men, twelve are found medically disqualified at MEPS and receive 4-F exemptions; four others are currently divinity students, gaining 2-D deferments; two request and are granted hardship deferments, and are 3-A; and the remaining two are appealing a local board denial of their claims for conscientious objector status. Since only those people who are both available **and eligible** can be inducted, no one from that community can be inducted because they are all either deferred, exempted, or using their appeal rights. These topics are all discussed in chapters below.

Order of priority for selection

Below are the various Selection Groups **in order of priority** for selection, together with a few remarks:

Volunteers: People between the ages of seventeen and twenty-five who volunteer to be drafted will be called before anyone else. The orders will be sent in the order in which people volunteered, regardless of age or lottery number. Volunteering for induction is not the same as enlisting. Volunteers are people who ask to be drafted but who do not actually sign up to go in. There have been two major reasons why people volunteer for the draft: First, being drafted means a two year stint in the military, while most enlistment contracts are for three or four years. Someone who chooses to go in but prefers to keep the time as short as possible may find volunteering a good option. Second, in many cases men facing criminal charges, especially draft law violators, have often been told that charges would be dropped if they entered the military. Many men have chosen two years in the military instead of the possibility of several years in prison.

Age Twenty Selection Group: After everyone in the Volunteers group has been called, the next group to be called upon is the Age Twenty Selection Group. This group includes everyone who turns twenty during the current year. This group is technically divided into two sub-groups. The first sub-group is men who were previously ordered for induction but who received a deferment or exemption (see Chapter 6). If the deferment or exemption expires while they are still in the Age Twenty Selection Group, they can be called for induction ahead of men who have never been called before.[5] But if a deferment or exemption expires after December 31, the man is not subject to being re-ordered—instead he will go into the Age Twenty-One Selection Group just as if he had never been called.[6] This is very different from the effect of a postponement (see Chapter 5): if you are called and get a postponement until after December 31, you can be rescheduled to report at the end of your postponement even if that occurs in a following calendar year.[7]

Age Twenty-One Selection Group: In the past, this group has been the promised land for men who don't want to get drafted. People in this group can be called only if everyone in the Age Twenty Selection Group has first been reached. It is possible that a declining birth rate coupled with a very large draft call could result in people in this group being called, but it seems unlikely. The relief only increases, as each year you rotate into a lower priority selection group.

Ages Twenty-two through Twenty-five Selection Group: These groups are for men who have already passed through the Age Twenty Selection Group and are currently dropping lower in priority with each passing year.

Ages Twenty-Six to Thirty-Four Selection Group: Draft liability ends entirely for most men once they have rotated out of the Age Twenty-Five Selection Group. The exceptions are those men who have previously been called and were given a deferment because of ROTC or similar training (Class 1-D-D), being a ministerial student (Class 2-D), because of dependents (Class 3-A), being an elected official (Class 4-B), or being found medically ineligible for the draft (Class 4-F). Those men will continue to drop down in Age Selection Groups until they have rotated out of the Age Thirty-Four Selection Group. Given the extreme unlikelihood of a draft big enough to reach even the Age Twenty-Two Selection Group, these lower groups are probably all but meaningless.

Age Nineteen and Age Eighteen-And-One-Half Selection Group: All but meaningless, as all of the higher age selection groups would have to be called first. In order for the draft to reach these groups, the world would have to be in deep, deep trouble.

ooo * ooo

Actually, the lottery system and the Order of Call are more complex than this explanation. It became so complex during the Vietnam war that local boards were continually messing up and placing people in the wrong priority group. Despite SS attempts to simplify the system, there will no doubt be numerous errors made in the future. Anyone having any questions regarding his lottery number or his priority should check carefully with a counselor or lawyer who is experienced in the technicalities of this area of draft law.

INDUCTION: WHAT
TO DO WHEN YOU ARE CALLED

For far too many men it is only the receipt of an induction order that causes them to finally start thinking about going into the military and what they want to do about it. Many see the induction order as an inescapable doom. While it is true that men who start thinking about the draft earlier have a better chance, receipt of an induction order is not the end of the line. Men who receive an induction order will still have a chance to gain deferment or exemption, provided that they act **very** quickly. I do not encourage men to wait until the last minute, but those who do should not feel that they are beyond hope.

There are basically four possible courses of action that a person with an induction order can take. You can (1) get your induction order cancelled or postponed, (2) accept induction into the military, (3) leave the country or go underground, or (4) refuse induction. Some of the choices are legal, while others are not. Nothing will make the whole mess go away, so a man with an induction order is going to need to decide quickly.

Postponement or cancellation

One possibility for someone with an induction order is to get the order cancelled or postponed. A man receiving an induction order will be allowed a brief period of time in which to request deferment or exemption.[1] Making such a request within the time limit should entitle you to at least a postponement of your induction date.[2] The only exception seems to be a claim for 4-F exemption (Chapter 12). Since 4-F status is determined by MEPS rather than the local board,[3] and since the pre-induction physical examination will be given on the date set for induction,[4] men claiming a 4-F exemption will most likely be instructed to bring their doctor's letter to MEPS on their scheduled induction date. However, if you claim any other deferment or exemption you might have your induction postponed or cancelled, or you could still be required to report for a physical exam on that date.

The law also provides that a full time high school or college student who receives an induction order may have his induction postponed until the end of the term.[5] High school students are entitled to a postponement until graduation from high school or age twenty, whichever occurs first. If you are a high school dropout, this is one more strong reason to go back for your diploma.

Any induction order which has not been legally issued must be cancelled. For instance, have you requested appeal rights, or do you still have time left to do so? Is the date to report for induction at least ten days after the mailing date of the induction order?[6] Is this your year of eligibility, and have you been placed in the correct Age Selection Group?[7] Have you presented a claim for deferment or exemption that forces the SS to reopen your classification and afford you new appeal rights?[8] You should never assume that your induction order is legal, but should have a counselor or lawyer check it for you. Many induction orders in the past have been found to be illegal. A man in that situation should immediately inform the SS of the illegality of the induction order and demand that the order be cancelled.

Even if an induction order is otherwise legal, the National Director of the SS has the authority to cancel or postpone induction in cases of death, serious illness or extreme emergency in your family.[9] The National SS Director also has the power to postpone your induction for almost any reason.[10] If you feel that you have a good reason for requesting postponement or cancellation of your induction order you might wish to contact your Area Office to explain in writing why your induction should be cancelled or postponed. At this point you have nothing to lose by trying. Your request should be sent by wire with a confirmation copy sent to yourself, or by Special Delivery mail, certified, return receipt requested.

Accepting induction

The simplest course of action is to accept induction. Some people who decide to accept induction have been able to adjust to the military environment with a minimum of problems. Others have found that the military is not for them, and many have been successful in obtaining various types of discharges after only a few weeks or months in the military. There are some points that should be considered by anyone who is thinking of accepting induction in order to try for a discharge. First, most reasons for discharge from the military are also reasons for deferment or exemption by the SS. It might make more sense for you to pursue classification through the SS rather than to go into the military in order to get out of the military. Another point is that going for a military discharge may be more difficult than being deferred or exempted by the SS, and may involve quite a bit more discomfort and emotional strain, as well as a lot of legal problems.

Since military law is very different from civilian law or Selective Service law, and since the military usually makes it difficult or impossible for inductees to get reliable counseling, it would be a good idea for anyone considering this alternative to do quite a bit of talking with a counselor or lawyer schooled in military law.

For some people, accepting induction may be the safest alternative. For instance, if your time limit for requesting deferment or exemption has already run out (or if you have lost all your appeals), you may be facing the choice of refusing induction followed by possible prosecution, or accepting induction. Likewise, a review of your file may show a strong possibility that you could be convicted of some other draft law violation, such as failure to provide a current address, to which you have no defense. In such situations many men prefer the choice of accepting induction for the purpose of seeking a military discharge, rather than to face an almost certain conviction should they refuse induction.

Even men with a seemingly good defense to a charge of refusing induction and no other possible charges, may choose to accept induction rather than face the possibility of being convicted in the courts and sent to prison. It is really a question of where you want to end up if you lose. If you refuse induction and lose, you may end up in prison. If you accept induction to seek discharge and lose, you will end up in the military. It is not an easy choice.

Requesting immediate discharge

The following procedures are suggested for anyone who decides to enter the military in order to try for a discharge. The sooner after entering the military that discharge is requested, the better the chances of having the request granted. It may be that the person who requests discharge the same day he is inducted will not get proper attention, in the belief that a few weeks in the military will "straighten him out". However, that procedure is probably illegal, and action can be taken if it occurs. The person who waits several weeks or months before applying for discharge runs the risk of having the military feel that he has already shown that he can function in the military (unless he has been AWOL or in some other way proved his unacceptability, which is not recommended since it could result in a military prison sentence).

Many people have had a great degree of success in applying for discharge the same day they were inducted. In most cases these people have been discharged within two or three months, and in some cases more quickly. The first point for a man in this situation to consider is his reason for requesting discharge. Unfortunately, the military does not hand out discharges to anyone who requests one. You must have a legal reason for your request, such as conscientious objection, erroneous induction, or so on.

To qualify for discharge as a conscientious objector you must show that your objection "crystallized" or changed substantially since your induction. There is also a provision for draftees who can show that a conscientious objector claim filed with the SS was improperly processed. People who file a request for discharge as a conscientious objector which is basically the same claim as the one the SS denied will not get a discharge.

Anyone who files for discharge as a conscientious objector **must** be placed on duty which provides the "minimum practicable conflict" with his beliefs.[11] This means that once you have filed, you cannot legally be

63

ordered to handle or train with weapons, or in any way violate your CO beliefs. Generally, the inductee who files for a conscientious objector discharge immediately after entering the military will be held at the Reception Station at the basic training base while his discharge application is processed. The "minimum conflict" clause remains effective until the conscientious objector claim has been finally approved or disapproved by the Pentagon.

To qualify for an erroneous induction discharge you must be able to show that you should not have been inducted in the first place; for example, if you were wrongfully denied a deferment or exemption; or, if you should not have been found qualified under the medical fitness standards; and so on.

As an example of erroneous induction, let's use the situation discussed in the chapter on medical exemptions—a man not qualified because of chronic athlete's foot.

On induction day, Dexter Ryan showed up with a rampant case of athlete's foot and three doctors' letters: one from two years previously, one from two months previously, and one dated four days before his induction date. He tried his best to fail the physical examination, but for some reason was found acceptable, and decided to accept induction. He does not meet the physical fitness standards, should not have been inducted, and therefore qualifies for an erroneous induction discharge.

Sometimes it works well to apply for discharge for several different reasons. For instance, let's say that in addition to his athlete's foot, entry into the military has also made Dexter realize that he is a conscientious objector. He can apply for an erroneous induction discharge because of his athlete's foot and for a conscientious objector discharge, both at the same time.

As soon as possible after induction Dexter should start looking for someone to present his discharge requests to. By the time he finally gets them into the right hands, half of the people on base are going to know that he is a "trouble maker" and the sooner they get rid of him the better it will be for the military.

Further, since Dexter is requesting discharge as a conscientious objector, the military is likely to feel that he may start "infecting" other recruits with his ideas. In no time at all he might have every recruit on the base filing for a conscientious objector discharge, and because of the "minimum conflict" rule, that would mean they could not conduct basic training, since none of them could be ordered to train with weapons. Not only is Dexter a trouble maker, he is a potential subversive as well! Hopefully, the military is going to realize they have nothing to gain and much to lose by keeping Dexter around, and will find the quickest, easiest way possible to get rid of him. Usually that would mean granting the erroneous induction discharge, but no matter which discharge request is granted, it will give him a discharge.

Often, of course, things don't go quite so smoothly as we might wish. It may be that both of Dexter's discharge requests are turned down. If so, he should be in touch with a civilian lawyer who handles military cases. In a great many cases he or she will be able to get Dexter discharged by filing a "habeas corpus petition" in federal court. In fact, Dexter may be wise to retain his attorney **before** entering the military. His lawyer can help prepare the discharge requests, and also help during the processing as well. If Dexter is filing for an erroneous induction discharge, his lawyer can file a habeas corpus petition on the day he accepts induction. That way, he can go directly to court without having to be processed by the military, which could save weeks or months of time. If he doesn't want an attorney, or would rather wait to see if he needs one, he should certainly work closely with a counselor who is familiar with military law.

Leaving the country

Another possibility is to move from the United States (or "go underground" within the US). This is a very big decision. Doing so is, of course, illegal. And unlike the Vietnam times, it seems likely that people choosing this option will not be given any form of amnesty or clemency in the future.

One of the problems with such a choice is that there are very few places left to go. Canada and Sweden, both sympathetic to US draft evaders during the Vietnam war, have let it be known that they no longer welcome draft evaders. Many foreign countries have a draft of their own, and US draft evaders moving to those countries could find themselves facing the draft in another country. Should a draft evader ever be deported from his new country back to the United States, he would most likely find a "welcoming committee" waiting for him: the FBI. If he left the United States and renounced his US citizenship, he would then be either a stateless person or an alien (citizen of another country). Under the regulations of the Immigration and Naturalization Service, he could be barred from ever re-entering the United States, even as a visitor.

Going underground has similar problems. If you get caught, a prosecution and conviction would be very likely. Even if not caught, the rigor of being a fugitive, establishing a new identity, avoiding old friends and acquaintances, and so on, can result in a paranoid and unpleasant existence.

There are many legal options available for avoiding the draft. Anyone considering leaving the country or going underground should think through his decision very carefully before making a move which could affect the rest of his life.

Refusing induction

This section is not intended to encourage anyone to refuse induction. Even in cases where a person may seem to have a legally sound reason for refusal, complications can arise which result in being convicted of a felony.

For thousands of people, the best answer to their draft problem seems to be to refuse induction into the military. This is especially true for people whose conscience will allow them to cooperate with the system to the point of attempting to gain some legal means of avoiding induction, but who feel that they cannot accept induction into the military under any circumstances. There are basically two ways to refuse induction: failing to report for induction when ordered, or reporting but refusing to submit to induction into the military.

Some people come to feel that to comply with the draft system in any way would be wrong, so they do not show up on their induction date. Usually the SS will give you another chance by sending a second reporting date. If that date is ignored as well, the FBI will likely be coming around looking for you, if they didn't come looking the first time. Unless they have an arrest warrant, you do not have to let them into your home or answer any of their questions. Perhaps the best thing to tell the FBI agents is that you will have your lawyer contact them, and that you have nothing further to say at that time. Do not get tricked into talking to them as they are just trying to make a case against you.

67

There are problems with a "no show" refusal of induction, especially since the man who is given another reporting date and still does not report may stand a higher chance of conviction than the man who reports but refuses induction.

Perhaps the cleanest way to refuse induction is to show up at the proper time and place, go through the pre-induction processing, but **refuse** to be inducted into the military. This way, you might be found unacceptable during the pre-induction physical examination and be given a 4-F exemption (see Chapter 12).

When ordered to report for induction you will be given a complete pre-induction physical examination on the day you report to the MEPS. Many people—roughly fifty percent of those who report—are found unacceptable at this point and given either a temporary or permanent medical disqualification.

If you are planning to avoid induction for medical, psychological or moral reasons, induction day will be your one big chance to be disqualified. You may want to let the examining doctors know that you plan to refuse induction if found qualified, and why. You also may want to ask the doctors for their names, in case you decide to sue them for medical malpractice should they find you acceptable. Men in this situation are advised to read Chapter 12. It may make the difference between being sent home with a 4-F exemption or having to refuse induction.

If you plan to refuse induction on grounds of conscience (such as if your conscientious objector claim was denied by the SS, or if you don't believe in the draft) you may wish to talk about your feelings at the MEPS. You never can tell what will happen. One person whose conscientious objector claim had been turned down decided to refuse induction. At the MEPS he took the time to explain his beliefs to everyone he met, to let them know that he was only there for the purpose of formally refusing induction. About half way through the processing an officer took him aside, listened to his entire story, and then sent him home. Two weeks later he received a new classification notice in the mail, with a 1-O classification on it. It isn't in the regulations, but it did work at least once.

Another person printed up a full page statement explaining that he felt the military was immoral, and proclaiming his intention to refuse induction. His statement also encouraged others concerned about the immorality of war and imperialism to refuse induction along with him. He handed out his flyers in front of the MEPS and spent the entire morning discussing the situation with anyone who would listen to him. He was found unacceptable for induction and sent home with a 4-F exemption. Again, a long shot, and a possibility of prosecution for encouraging others to violate the law. But it did work at least once.

Much of the induction process involves filling out papers and standing in lines. The important moment comes when you are taken to a large room for the actual induction ceremony. Everyone will be lined up and told to step forward when their name is called. **Don't** take that step if you plan to refuse induction!

It **is the act of stepping forward that constitutes induction.** Contrary to popular belief, taking the oath of induction occurs **after** induction, and refusing to take the oath is punishable under military law, since you are already in the military by that time.

If you plan to refuse induction, you should not step forward when your name is called. Just to make sure that there is no question about it, you should also say out loud that you refuse induction. There is no danger of anyone pushing you forward or anything like that; it is just that you want to make sure the officials understand what you are doing. Sometimes people in the Army aren't too bright.

If you refuse to take the step forward, an Army officer will probably take you quickly into a private room. After all, they don't want you infecting others with your weird ideas. You will likely be told the penalty for refusing induction is five years in jail and a ten thousand dollar fine, that it is a federal felony offense, and that you will be sent to prison if you refuse induction. The Army will do everything in their power to scare you. Then, they will probably offer you another chance to step forward. I am sure we can all appreciate their thoughtfulness.

If you resist their efforts to get you to step forward, they will probably ask you to make or sign a statement that you have willfully refused induction. I strongly recommend that you **refuse** to make such a statement. If you do give such a statement, it is an admission or confession which can be used against you in a court of law. It is never a good idea to admit that you are guilty of any crime, at least not until you have consulted a lawyer.

After refusing induction you may be arrested. People are usually just told to go home, and that they will be contacted later, but every once in a while a person is actually taken from the induction center to a police station for booking. If you are arrested on the spot, you will probably be let go on your own recognizance after booking, unless they have reason to think you may not show up, or unless they are in a bad mood. Being released without bail means they trust you to show up for trial. However, just in case the police do decide to hold you, you should arrange for bail ahead of time. It would be a good idea for you to write the phone number of your lawyer, friend or bail bondsman on your arm with a ballpoint pen before induction. That way, even if the police take away your clothing and your wallet (a common booking procedure) you will still have the phone number handy.

What happens after refusal

After induction processing has been completed, all files are returned to the SS. The files of those who have refused induction will be forwarded to the United States Attorney's office, where a decision will be made whether or not the government wants to prosecute. The US Attorney will usually not bring charges unless he feels he can win the case. Even though the US Attorney screens cases pretty thoroughly, it is interesting to note that in the past not all people were convicted, and not all convictions resulted in prison sentences. Of those who were taken to court, well over half were found not guilty. For example, in the fiscal year ended June 30, 1971, there were 2,973 Selective Service cases that got to court. While that was a higher number than in any year since 1945, only 34.8% were convicted, and of those convicted only 36% were sent to prison. So, only about 13% of the court cases resulted in a person being sent to prison.[12] Of course, the figures could be different next time around, and statistics don't help if you are the one guy in one hundred who ends up in the slam. Still, the figures are interesting. For more on this see Chapter 17.

There is another thing that you should consider if you are thinking of refusing induction. You can be taken to court on more than one charge. The US Attorney's policy during the later Vietnam era seemed to be moving toward a position of trying to convict people, regardless of the charge, if they refused induction. In other words, even if the government couldn't make the charge of "refusing induction" stick, they were just as happy to nab people on some other charge, such as late registration or failure to report an address change. There have even been cases of people being acquitted of refusing induction, and then being taken back into court on some other charge and convicted.

If the government decides not to prosecute, you may get a letter from either the US Attorney or your local board, instructing you to report at once to your local board office. Upon reporting you may be informed of the decision not to prosecute, or you may be told that a previously denied classification will be reconsidered by the board.

Another possibility is that you may simply be sent a new classification from your local board. Usually, if you are reclassified by the local board after refusing induction, you are well on the way to the classification you want. In many cases the board will simply send it to you, but sometimes you will be sent a new 1-A classification and will have to start your appeal process all over again. In rare cases even the second appeal may be shot down, and you may once again end up with an induction order. One person I know got seven induction orders before his local board finally gave in and granted him a 1-O classification.

If the US Attorney decides to prosecute, there may be a warrant issued for your arrest. You or your lawyer can check this out by calling the US Marshall's office and asking if there is a warrant out in your name. In some cities the Marshall is very civil about the entire affair. An officer will call on the phone to ask if you would like to come down and surrender. If you agree, they will usually book you and then release you on your own recognizance. But just in case the Marshall in your area isn't so considerate, you or your lawyer should check from time to time to see if a warrant has been issued. If so, you might call them and offer to surrender.

If you don't surrender, or are not given the opportunity to do so, the Marshals will come looking for you. There is nothing more inconvenient than being rousted out of bed at three in the morning just to be arrested . . . or being arrested on a Friday night and not being able to raise bail or see a magistrate until Monday morning. It's much more tolerable to deal with the police at a civilized time of day, and on your own terms.

Another way to avoid unnecessary hassle over being arrested might be for you or your lawyer to send a letter (certified, return receipt, of course) to the Marshall's office explaining that you are willing to surrender to any warrant if the Marshall will just be good enough to give a call or send a letter and let you know when and where to surrender.

Looking for a lawyer

If you are going to refuse induction you will probably need a lawyer. You could choose to defend yourself, but in my experience, judges tend to be harsher on defendants who insist on representing themselves.

The first person to ask about a good draft lawyer is your draft counselor. The counselor may be a lawyer or may be able to refer you to a good one. In many areas of the country there are groups of lawyers who specialize in handling Selective Service cases. Those people are usually quite good in their area of law, and are sometimes able to take cases for relatively low fees if you are not able to pay the full fee. Lawyers' fees will vary. Some lawyers charge an hourly rate, while others charge a flat fee. Some charge very little, while others charge quite a lot. There is a saying that you get what you pay for. To some extent this is true with lawyers, although it might be more accurate to say that you pay for what you get. The more skillful draft lawyers usually have a good reputation and can afford to charge higher fees for their services, but there are a lot of excellent lawyers who don't charge big fees. Even though an expensive lawyer may be a good lawyer, it doesn't necessarily follow that a less expensive lawyer is not.

Another point to keep in mind is that lawyers, like all professionals, tend to specialize in one or two fields. A person certainly wouldn't go to a dentist for a stomach ache, or call the plumber if the lights went out, so why hire a civil lawyer for a draft case? You should make sure that the lawyer you hire knows a great deal about draft law. The best way to be sure of this is to hire a lawyer who handles a lot of draft cases. Such lawyers are likely to be well known to the draft counselors in their area.

Do **not** depend on father's lawyer just because he has always done well for father. After all, father isn't getting drafted, is he? The lawyer may be a real whiz at handling taxes and civil law suits, but he may know less about draft law than you do.

The decision of whether to accept or refuse induction is not simple, nor is it easy. There are a lot of things to be considered, and your final decision could affect your life for quite a while to come. It is unfortunate that such choices are forced on people, and yet the decision is there and cannot be ignored. You should decide well ahead of time what you are going to do if ordered for induction. A decision made in the heat of the moment is unlikely to be well thought out.

CLASSIFICATION
EXEMPTIONS AND DEFERMENTS

At present no one is being classified. Under the current regulations no one will be classified until drafting begins, but that could happen very suddenly, at any time. When drafting does begin, **all** draft registrants will be **presumed** to be classified 1-A for purposes of sending out induction orders.[1]

As soon as a draft is ordered, local boards and area offices will quickly go into action, induction orders will begin going out, and the classification process will begin immediately.

Men who report for induction without claiming any deferment or exemption will never be assigned to a local board. For those who do claim a deferment or exemption, the SS will set up individual files.[2] A man's draft file will contain any information he submits, such as applications for deferment or exemption, as well as any other information the SS has on him, such as results of physical examinations at MEPS, information about him submitted by other people, and so on. There was a time when the SS was required to keep **anything** a registrant sent them, but people started sending in old tires, bricks, packages of garbage, and so on. The regulations were quickly changed, and when local boards resume operations they will be authorized to throw away anything that is considered irrelevant or duplicative. In other words, they will not be required to keep that 4' x 8' piece of plywood you send them, unless, of course, it has your conscientious objector application written on it, in which case they will probably be required to keep it. And they will probably find a reason to deny your claim for conscientious objector status as well.

Bear in mind that under current regulations all draft registrants will be presumed to be classified 1-A **unless** they submit a claim for deferment or exemption. Also bear in mind that once you are ordered for induction, your claim **must** be submitted **before** the date you are supposed to report to MEPS. If you do not make the claim within that very short period, you will have given up your right to make the claim at all.[3] Information on how to make a claim, and the forms to use in making a claim, will be made available if inductions begin. Since there is no requirement that you use any specific form, the information contained in this book is really all you need, and probably a lot better than anything the SS would make available.

Deferments and exemptions

Each draft registrant will be placed into one of eighteen classifications, and his classification will determine whether or not he is subject to being drafted.

Whenever the system classifies anyone (other than the "presumed" 1-A), there is a procedure set out in the SS regulations that they must follow. If you claim to be eligible for any deferment or exemption, especially if you claim conscientious objector status or a dependency deferment, the SS **must** send you the appropriate forms and allow you time to fill out and return them.[4]

Your order to report to MEPS may be cancelled or postponed if you file for a deferment or exemption, or you may be instructed to report to MEPS for physical examination only, but not for induction into the military.

If you claim one of the five Judgmental Classifications (1-A-O, 1-O, 2-D, 3-A, or 4-D) your file will be sent to the local board for the area that contains the **permanent address** which you have given to the SS.[5] Claims for conscientious objector status will **automatically** be set up for your personal appearance before the board,[6] but claims for other classes will be heard in your absence unless you expressly ask for a personal appearance.[7]

If your claim is for one of the Administrative Classifications (see list below) the claim will be reviewed by the area office.[8] If the area office denies the claim you may appeal to the local board and may request a personal appearance before the board to argue your claim.[9]

You may claim more than one classification. For instance, you may feel entitled to a conscientious objector classification, a dependency deferment, a divinity student deferment, and a physical exemption. If so, you have an absolute right to claim them all. The law states that you **must** be considered for and placed in the **lowest** classification for which you qualify.[10]

Listed below are the eighteen classifications that Selective Service uses, along with a short explanation of what each classification means and reference to the parts of this book where it is discussed more fully. The list is in order of priority as established by the SS; that is, 1-A is the highest priority, the first to go, and 1-H is the lowest and last. Remember, if you qualify for more than one classification on this list you must be given the one which is **lowest** on the list.

1-A Fully eligible for induction into military service. **All** draft registrants will be **presumed** 1-A. Those in the Age Twenty Selection Group with low lottery numbers will be ordered for induction first and then allowed a short time in which to claim some other classification.

1-A-O Conscientious objector willing to go into military service as a non-combatant, but not as a combatant member. (Chapter 7; Judgmental.)

1-O Conscientious objector opposed to any kind of military service, but willing to do civilian work contributing to the national health, safety or interest. (Chapter 7; Judgmental.)

2-D Student of theology satisfactorily pursuing studies preparing him for the ministry. (Chapter 10; Judgmental.)

3-A Registrant with one or more dependents whose dependents would suffer hardship economically, physically or emotionally if he were drafted. (Chapter 8; Judgmental.)

4-D Full time or regularly practicing minister of religion. (Chapter 10; Judgmental.)

1-D-D ROTC students, men who have accepted a reserve officer standby commission, aviation cadet applicants, and men who have enlisted in a military reserve component. (Chapter 11; Administrative.)

4-B Judges and certain federal and state elected officials. (Chapter 11; Administrative.)

78

4-C Non-US citizens and dual nationals who are exempt from the draft, currently outside the US, or have been in the US less than one year. (Appendix A; Administrative.)

4-G Person whose father, brother or sister died as a result of injury or disease incurred while in the military. (Chapter 9; Administrative.)

4-A People who have already served in the military, including non-US citizens and dual citizens of some countries who have completed military service in their own country. (Chapter 11, Appendix A; Administrative.)

4-W Conscientious objector (1-O) who has completed civilian alternate service work. (Chapter 7; Administrative.)

1-D-E Students enrolled in an officer procurement program at an approved military college; men in the Delayed Entry Program of military enlistments; certain military reservists. (Chapter 11; Administrative.)

1-C Active duty military members, commissioned officers of the Public Health Service or the National Oceanic and Atmospheric Administration. (Chapter 11; Administrative).

1-W Conscientious objector (1-O) currently performing civilian alternate service. (Chapter 7; Administrative).

4-T Non-US citizens exempt from the draft under a treaty between the US and the citizen's country. (Appendix A; Administrative).

4-F Person found by MEPS to be not qualified for military service or service as a conscientious objector because of medical, mental or administrative reasons. (Chapters 12, 13; Administrative).

1-H Administrative "holding" classification for people whose age group is not being currently called, or whose lottery number is above the announced ceiling. (Chapter 11; Administrative).

The SS likes to give the public the impression that 1-A is the classification they give men only if they can't find any other classification they qualify for. But the fact of the matter is that their job is to draft people. Members of a board would quickly be asked to resign (or perhaps even be prosecuted) if they were primarily interested in granting a deferment or exemption to everyone who came along. If you want a classification other than 1-A, you can probably get it, but you may have to work for it, and for some of you it may be very hard work.

In the following chapters, there is a detailed discussion of the various exemptions and deferments, with tips on how to get the one you want. Chapter 14 tells you what to do if you don't get your way.

CONSCIENTIOUS OBJECTION

One of the most talked-about aspects of the draft is Conscientious Objection, commonly called CO status. It seems that just about everyone knows that there is such a thing, but very few people understand what it is really all about.

Some people seem to think that filing for CO status is an easy and automatic was to "get out" of the draft. If you have read this far, you know that the SS is not about to give people an easy way out. Conscientious objectors are subject to being drafted. The difference is that a man drafted as a CO doesn't have to put in two years as a combat member of the military.

Many people believe that conscientious objector status stems from the First Amendment guarantees of freedom of religion. Unfortunately, that belief is incorrect; the US Supreme Court ruled long ago that there is no such constitutional right.[1] It exists only because the draft law, passed by Congress, allows it to exist.[2] It is very doubtful that Congress would decide to discontinue conscientious objector status, but it is scary to know that it could happen.

Conscientious objections in other countries

Presently there are only four countries in the world that constitutionally guarantee conscientious objec-

81

tion to military service: West Germany, the Netherlands, Austria, and Finland. Costa Rica endorses it, but it is not a constitutional right. Provisions for COs do exist in many other countries by way of statutes or administrative decrees.

Both the Consultative Assembly of the Council of Europe and the European Parliament have passed resolutions calling for the right to refuse armed military service on grounds of conscience. Of course, these are merely recommendations to the member states of the European Community and do not guarantee rights for COs.

In this country we take it for granted that we can go to a draft counselor or read a book like this to obtain information on conscientious objection. But the situation in other countries can run from bad to dismal. In France, even though a CO provision was granted in 1963, it was also illegal until 1983 for anyone to publish or distribute literature that referred to the statute. In Greece only Jehovah Witnesses are recognized as COs; other objectors are serving repeated prison sentences, fleeing their homes, or seeking asylum in other countries. In El Salvador induction into the armed forces may consist of forced enlistment through abduction from the streets. The individual's conscience is not part of the consideration.

What is conscientious objection?

To qualify for classification as a conscientious objector a person must show that his deeply and sincerely held religious, moral or ethical beliefs cause him to feel opposed to taking part in all war in any form.[3] Naturally it isn't quite as easy as just writing that sentence on a piece of paper and sending it to a draft board, but that definition sums it up in a nutshell.

A conscientious objector is subject to being called in the same way as other draft registrants: his lottery number must be reached while he is a member of the Age Group being called (see Chapter 4) and he must be found physically acceptable.[4] The physical fitness standards for conscientious objectors are exactly the same as for 1-A draftees, and since the 4-F medical exemption is a lower classification than either of the conscientious objector classifications (see Chapter 6), anyone who is found to be physically unacceptable doesn't have to worry about qualifying as a CO because he can't be drafted anyway.[5] But a conscientious objector who qualifies for no other deferment or exemption will be subject to the draft.

There are two conscientious objector classifications used by the SS: 1-A-O and 1-O. When filing for CO status a man is supposed to choose one or the other. Some people do not feel that they can accept either classification, since neither one really defines their feelings, or since they object to the "right" of the SS to classify people at all. While these are admirable and valid opinions, CO claims based on such reasons are not likely to be approved. Any conscientious objector who feels that he can not accept either CO classification offered by the SS should work closely with a lawyer.

1-A-O and 1-O conscientious objectors

A 1-A-O classification is available for those conscientious objectors who object to taking part in combat, but are willing to enter the military in some non-combatant job.[5] Of the two CO classifications, the 1-A-O is the easier to get, since a 1-A-O draftee will go into the military and thereby fill the draft quota. However, no one should request 1-A-O status simply because it is easier to obtain—you should file only for the status you really want. While both classifications require similar kinds of proof, a 1-A-O who later requests 1-O status stands a poor chance of success, and in fact could even lose his 1-A-O status in the process.

If granted 1-A-O status, a man will go into the military as a non-combatant. He will still have to go through complete military training and orientation, but will not be given arms training and will not be forced to bear arms. In addition, he will be trained to do a non-combat military job. The overwhelming majority of 1-A-O draftees during Vietnam were trained to be medics.

There is absolutely nothing in draft or military law to keep a 1-A-O from being sent into a combat zone or working on the front lines. If he has been trained as a medic, the odds are extremely high that that is precisely where he will end up. After all, that is where medics are needed.

The basic differences between being drafted as a 1-A draftee or as a 1-A-O is that the 1-A-O will not have to carry or use firearms. Both are in uniform, both are sworn to support the military and its missions, and both are subject to all military rules and regulations. The 1-A-O will not be called upon to kill, but there is nothing to prevent him from being injured or killed.

Some conscientious objectors feel that they can enter the military as medics because it is a humanitarian job to assist the wounded. For other objectors, a close look at the realities of being a part of a war effort causes them to take a different view. In medic school, for example, one is taught that the job of a medic is to patch up soldiers, not necessarily to heal their wounds, but to send them out to fight again. The military medic policy is often to treat the **least injured** first, since they have the best chance of a speedy return to battle.

Many conscientious objectors feel that there is no real difference between ordering bombs and dropping them, or between killing someone and assisting someone else to kill them. For conscientious objectors who feel that they can not serve in the military in any way, there is the 1-O classification.[6]

If drafted as a 1-O, a man will be called for the same period of time as anyone else who is drafted--two years. The big difference is that instead of being called for military duty, a 1-O is required to perform two years of civilian work that is approved by the SS. This is known as civilian alternate service work.[7] Many of the approvable jobs are very menial and uncreative, such as working as a hospital orderly, driving a truck for Goodwill Industries, and so on. But there are some decent jobs which a 1-O can have approved, and upon being ordered into civilian alternate service work a 1-O has an opportunity to locate his own job and submit it to the SS for approval.[8]

Of course, being drafted as a 1-O is still being drafted. But to many people being drafted to work in the civilian community for two years seems a whole lot better than being drafted to carry a gun and fight.

Who qualifies as a CO?

A conscientious objector is someone whose conscience would give him no peace if he took part in warfare. In the past only "religious objectors" were recognized. If a man wasn't a member of a recognized "peace church," such as the Quakers or Mennonites, he was pretty much out of luck. But two important Supreme Court decisions[9] have expanded the meaning of the word "religious" to include any strongly held moral or ethical belief. In other words, you no longer have to belong to a church or believe in a God to be classified as a conscientious objector, as long as you feel very strongly that participation in war is wrong. The Supreme Court definition of a conscientious objector is someone whose deeply and sincerely held religious, moral or ethical beliefs cause him to be opposed to taking part in all war in any form.[10]

If you think the above definition may apply to you, then I strongly recommend that you read the **Handbook for Conscientious Objectors**, published by the Central Committee for Conscientious Objectors (address in Appendix B). That book contains many good thoughts on the issue of "selective" objection, objection to nuclear war, and so on. Also remember rule #8 at the front of this book: when in doubt, file a claim.

People who feel that a particular war or particular kind of war (such as oil wars, nuclear wars, and so on) is wrong, but feel that they would fight in some other wars, do not qualify as conscientious objectors under current law.[11] Also, anyone whose reasons for objecting to war are political (the US has no right to be an imperialist nation), sociological (it is wrong for this society to waste its healthy men) or pragmatic (I don't want to get injured or killed) are not qualified as conscientious objectors.[12] Those may be valid views which would cause a person to be opposed to war, but the SS won't accept those reasons as a basis for a CO claim.

If a person feels morally compelled to push for "selective objection" to a particular war, or political conscience as a basis for a CO claim, more power to him. But be aware that others have tried it before, and many ended up in jail for their beliefs.

A person need not be a pacifist to qualify as a conscientious objector. Conscientious objectors may believe in self-defense or defense of their loved ones, but still be opposed to taking part in war.[13] It is not necessary to convince the SS that your beliefs are **right**, but only that you sincerely hold those beliefs and live by them. One man who was born and raised on a Pacific island based his CO claim on the belief that God lived in a volcano on his homeland. The local board may not have been converted to his religious beliefs, but they did find him to sincerely hold those beliefs and granted his 1-O request.

The SS has a form to be filled out by conscientious objectors. It contains questions about the applicant's beliefs and how those beliefs relate to his feelings about war. The questions are not easy to answer, and may take weeks or even months of consideration. There are no "right" answers, since each person's beliefs are going to be slightly different. But there are some "wrong" answers, in the sense that some kinds of responses will virtually assure a denial of a claim.

Putting together a conscientious objector application that is complete and accurately expresses your belief can be a long and difficult task. Remember that if the draft is fired up without warning you might find yourself with only a couple of weeks to get your claim written and submitted. Throwing together an application under the pressure of a ten or fifteen day deadline could result in a denial of an otherwise valid claim. If you intend to file as a conscientious objector it would be very wise to start working on your claim right now.

The SS form has changed over the years and is likely to keep changing in the future. Your draft counselor (see Forward and Appendix B) will probably have a copy of the most recent form, along with literature about conscientious objection. He can also help you to think through your feelings about war and to put together an application for CO status that will avoid the more common pitfalls. With some help, you may stand a better chance with your claim.

The questions

Despite the changes to the SS form over the years, there are four basic areas that will almost certainly be explored in any CO application. Even if the form does not specifically ask for the following information you should be prepared to provide it, because all four areas are essential parts of a CO claim.

A. What are your beliefs?

This kind of question asks you to describe the religious, moral, or ethical beliefs that underlie your objection to taking part in war. Do you believe in a God? If so, what are the teachings of your God? Do you belong to a religious organization? If so, what are its teachings? If you do not believe in a God, what code of ethics or morals do you use to guide your life?

In approaching this area of questions, many people fall into the trap of discussing only their beliefs about war. Naturally, you are going to want to discuss that, but try not to confine yourself to only that issue. Include a discussion of **all** your beliefs. For instance, a member of a traditional Christian religion could not only point to his church's official statement in support of conscientious objection, but could also discuss his belief in the Ten Commandments, the Golden Rule, the teachings of the Sermon on the Mount, and so on. Those things may not have anything to do with conscientious objection to war, but they help to make the important point that the person has a broad base of beliefs which guide his life in many ways, including the issue of war.

B. Which kind of C.O. are you?

It is up to you to inform the SS whether your beliefs cause you to object only to combatant military service (Class 1-A-O) or to all military service no matter what the job (Class 1-O). If your claim is for noncombatant status you may want to explain why your beliefs cause you to oppose participation in all war, but still allow you to enter the military as a noncombatant. This can be a ticklish area, because an objection to personally being harmed is not a legal basis for CO status. In other words, if you object to combat because you might get shot, it won't work; but if you object to combat because shooting someone would violate your conscience, that will qualify.

For the 1-O objector this area gets equally difficult. This is where you must show that **any** participation in the military—whether directly combatant or noncombatant—would violate your beliefs. This can involve some very fine points. For instance, if you really are opposed to supporting the machinery of war, why do you pay income taxes when over half the national budget pays for military personnel and weapons? What is wrong with being a cook or a supply sergeant?

C. Where did your beliefs come from?

This is largely a historical area, wanting to know what life experiences have led you to believe as you do. Have you received formal religious training? Even if you do not belong to a religious organization, do you believe in some or all of the teachings of a particular religion? Have your beliefs been influenced by books you have read, classes you have taken in school, or people you have known? Bear in mind that this area asks not only for the development of your beliefs about war, but all of your religious, moral, or ethical beliefs which you discussed in the first area.

89

An important consideration in this area is: when did your beliefs cause you to become opposed to participating in war? Have you felt that way for as long as you can remember, or did you never really think about it until recently? Local boards are not supposed to deny a claim only because someone's conscientious objection is a recent development.[14] By the same token, the guy who can point to a long history of beliefs may be more believable than someone whose objection is newly formed. The more background you can show, the stronger your claim will be.

D. What shows that you are sincere?

This is probably the most difficult area to answer, but it may also be the most important. The most common reason for denying CO claims during the Vietnam era was that the board did not believe the applicant to be sincere. You should be prepared to demonstrate that you live by the beliefs you have described.

Some people state that their application for CO status shows that their beliefs are deeply held. Not only is this logic questionable, but the frequency with which that statement pops up causes boards to be bored with it.

In approaching this area, try to describe events in your life that show that you live consistently with your beliefs. For instance, if you believe in the Ten Commandments, you could demonstrate incidents in your life showing that you do not take the Lord's name in vain, that you honor your parent's, that you do not covet your neighbor's property. . . . and, of course, that you do not kill. If you belong to a church, you can show that you attend worship ceremonies and abide by the teachings of that church.

There are two common stories that may illustrate the kinds of incidents that can be used in this

91

area of questioning. First, the hunting story. Sometimes a budding CO first realizes what it means to kill when he goes hunting. Some people "freeze up" and find themselves unable to pull the trigger. Others are able to shoot, but then feel guilt or remorse for what they have done. In either case, those people realize that they can not kill even birds or animals, let alone another human being.

The other is the "stealing story." Some people have stolen something, often something petty like a candy bar when they were kids, and then felt their conscience telling them that what they have done is wrong. Others are given an opportunity to be dishonest but find that they can not do it. Those experiences show that a person's beliefs about honesty are deeply and sincerely held, and that is the name of the game.

Naturally, there are lots of other stories that can fit under this heading: stories of schoolyard fights, helping little old ladies across the street, stopping to help motorists with automobile trouble, and so on. Anything that tends to show you take your beliefs seriously can be used.

One further word of caution about filling out CO forms: the SS has usually designed the form to encourage brief, one-paragraph answers, or even just check-box answers. **Don't fall for it!** Your claim is probably not complete enough unless you have written at least one or two pages in response to each of the questions discussed above. Many COs have found that even that is not enough space for what they need to say. Naturally, quality is far more important than quantity, and it is possible for an application to be too long. Boards are unlikely to carefully read a forty page application. The important thing is not to feel compelled to fit your answers into a small one-paragraph format.

For further information about the actual filing process, and for help in thinking through your potential answers, see a draft counselor. An excellent discussion of conscientious objection can be found in the "Handbook for Conscientious Objectors" published by the Central Committee for Conscientious Objection whose addresses are in the back of this book. This is strongly recommended reading for anyone interested in the subject.

When to file

The current regulations seem designed to make it very difficult for you to file a CO claim. You can not file until **after** you have been sent an order to report for induction.[15] You must then file your application **before** the date set for you to report to MEPS[16] which could be as little as ten days from the date the order was sent. If you do not file within that very brief period, you may have given up all chance of filing at all.[17]

You will not be required to file a complete CO claim in that brief period, but you will have to file something **in writing** requesting to be considered for conscientious objector status. In response, a form may be sent to you that same day, and you may be given as little as **ten days** in which to return your complete written application.[18] In other words, you will probably have less than nineteen days between the time you are **sent** an induction order and the time you must submit your complete claim. The earlier you start working on your claim, the better your chances for meeting that deadline with a successful application.

Even though the Registration Form does not have a box to check for conscientious objection, you may still wish to register as a CO, or to inform the SS of your beliefs after you have registered but before you are ordered for induction. When you go to the post office to register, you could take a broad-tipped felt pen with you. Find some available space on the registration form and simply write in the words, "I am a conscientious objector." You can do this if you are a CO, or if you think you might become one, or even if you are unsure if you are one or not. By doing this, you have at least begun to set up some documentation for a CO claim.

Some COs have used the postage-paid Change of Information Form available in post offices to inform the SS that they are COs. Still others have written letters to the SS explaining their beliefs, or have submitted complete written applications. While none of these things are provided for in the regulations, proof that you have done one or more of them could help bolster the "sincerity" and "depth of conviction" parts of your claim if and when you do receive an induction order. Please do not forget that none of these unofficial ways of indicating your CO beliefs will be enough by themselves. If you receive an induction order, or if you are given any other official means for notifying the SS, you must **strictly** follow all the official procedures and meet all deadlines in order to insure that your claim will be heard.

Alternate service work

Despite the fact that most alternate service work tends to be menial and low-paying or non-paying, there are redeeming factors. For one thing, if you obtain a 1-O classification, you will be given a chance to locate a job that you want to do, and submit it to the SS for approval.[19] Believe it or not, there are some approved or approvable jobs that aren't too bad, and a few that are very good. Some civil service positions are approved, free clinics sometimes qualify, some forms of social work, especially in poor or minority communities, may qualify, and there are even some approved jobs working in foreign countries with religious or social groups.

94

In addition to "traditionally approved" jobs, the SS is always open to new jobs, so even if the job you would like to do has never before been approved, it may be that you and your prospective employer can present the job to the SS in a way that will get the system to approve it.

Almost all approved alternate service jobs pay very little, since they are required to be in the national health, safety or interest, which usually translates into working for a non-profit organization. But there are at least some jobs where a person can feel creative and positive. In the past, some counseling agencies have had CO job counseling available, including lists of approved or potentially approvable jobs in the area.

If you are called for alternate service work and do not find an acceptable job the SS will assign you a job.[21] You can bet that if you wait for a "work order" to be issued you are going to be assigned to the lousiest job they can come up with. If you refuse to comply with a work order, you can be prosecuted just the same as if you had refused to comply with an induction order.[22] The difference is that people convicted of refusing to comply with a work order stand a stronger chance of being sent to prison than those who refuse induction. Apparently the courts feel that a conscientious objector has already "been given a break". You may request postponement of a work order on the same basic grounds as are used for a postponement of induction.[23]

In the past it was worth bearing in mind that a work order to a specific job didn't necessarily mean that there was work available with that employer. Many times people under work orders travelled hundreds of miles to comply, only to find that the employer had no position available. One way to avoid being ripped off by the SS like that is to explain to the local board that you will

95

comply with the order, but that you can't afford the travel expenses. Several objectors have used that to insist that their local board arrange for their transportation when they have been ordered to a place distant from their place of residence. They sometimes further demanded that the SS guarantee them, in writing, that return passage will be paid by the SS if work is not available at that location for at least six weeks. Some boards found it easier to cancel the work order than to comply with the regulations.

Of those boards that did guarantee transportation cost requests, some had occasion to get upset when some CO would show up thoroughly refreshed by his vacation, demanding return bus fare because there was no job available. There have even been reports that some conscientious objectors did not even bother to take the trip. They cashed in their bus ticket (paid for by the SS) and placed a long-distance call to the employer. When told that the employer was not hiring, they asked that he or she send them a letter to that effect. When they got the letter, they took it to their local board and demanded return bus fare. Such a practice is, of course, highly illegal and should not be done. It is not nice to rip off the SS for a couple hundred dollars, and besides, you might get caught and go to jail for doing it.

Other objectors, especially those who were gainfully employed when ordered to report for alternate service work, seemed to find great difficulty in getting hired by an alternate service employer. They reported for job after job, but kept getting turned down. That is not difficult to understand, since many Vietnam-era objectors were dirty hippies who never bathed or shaved, and always wore old tattered clothing. I mean, would you want your sister to work with one? Heavens, no! Fortunately for some objectors, neither did some employers.

The SS is attempting to combat that situation by having a regulation enacted that says you can be prosecuted if your employer fires you because of your appearance.[24] It is questionable whether the SS can legally dictate your appearance, although the safer route may be not to challenge them. The regulation does not cover being refused a job, only being fired once you have started one.

During Vietnam days, the scarcity of jobs in California and Washington for conscientious objectors and the inability of some objectors to be hired was countered by the establishment of an "Ecology Corps". Several old prison camps were re-opened and staffed, sometimes by prison guards. While the name "Ecology Corps" seemed to imply a concern for the environment, these camps were actually just a cheap way to procure fire-fighters. Reports from objectors in the California Ecology Corps indicated that they were more like prison camps or concentration camps than the "volunteer" organizations they were supposed to be. There were some reports of brutality, and many reports of forced hair-cutting. The SS apparently approved of the Ecology Corps experiment, because current alternate regulations set up a complex system for the SS to maintain a pool of eligible employers.[25]

There are procedures for requesting job reassignment if you are unable to continue working for your alternate service employer. Some reasons for such a request might be that your job violates your CO beliefs,[26] that bad health incapacitates you,[27] or that you have "continual and severe differences" with your employer.[28] If your reassignment request is denied, you can appeal the decision to a Civilian Review Board.[29] An appeal must be in writing, and must be filed within fifteen days of denial.[30] If you request it in writing you have a right to appear to present your case, but there is

97

no right to present witnesses or to be represented by counsel at the hearing.[31]

An interesting twist in the alternate service regulations says that if a dependency situation develops after you begin alternate service work you can get your work order suspended.[32] The requirements for a work order suspension are exactly the same as for a 3-A Dependency classification (see Chapter 8). The catch is this: if you get a normal 3-A classification that lasts through your period in the Age Twenty Selection Group, you automatically rotate into the next age group at the end of the year and are unlikely to be called again.[33] Likewise, if you had entered the military and then qualified for a 3-A, you would be discharged from military service.[34] However, if you get a suspension from alternate service work on the dependency basis, then you can be ordered back to work if your suspension is terminated before you reach the Age Twenty-Six Selection Group! That policy will undoubtedly be challenged in the courts someday if the SS tries to enforce it.

There are ways you can be released from alternate service work before your two years are up. If you qualify for a 4-F exemption (see Chapters 12 and 13) either before or after you begin work, you will be given a release.[35] You can also be released up to thirty days early if you are enrolled in school and scheduled to start classes just before your two year period ends,[36] or if you have a job lined up that will not wait.[37]

While engaged in alternate service you will be classified 1-W.[38] Once you have satisfactorily completed alternate service you will be classified 4-W.[39]

Some points for COs to consider

The processing of a claim for CO status is basically the same as the processing of any claim

98

requesting deferment or exemption. Since both the 1-A-O and 1-O classifications are judgmental, the claim will be decided by your local board. However, CO applicants do not have a choice over whether or not to attend the hearing: a personal appearance before the board is **required** in all CO cases.[40] If for any reason you do not attend the hearing, it **must** be rescheduled. If you do not attend the rescheduled hearing, you claim will be dismissed and you will have no right of appeal.[41] For more information about claims processing be sure to read Chapters 14, 15, and 16.

You should be sure to take advantage of all of your appeal rights, for several reasons:

1) Any time that you fail to make full use of your appeal rights, you are limiting the chances of having your claim granted.

2) By not showing up for a personal appearance with the local board, or by not requesting a district appeal, you may bring question on your sincerity as a CO.

3) The courts are sometimes called upon to review CO claims. That usually happens after an objector's claim is denied and he has been ordered for induction, but he refuses to be inducted. As a defense, it is possible to argue that the induction order should not have been issued, since the man should have been classified 1-O, and of course a 1-O is not inducted. However, the courts have a rule that before they will look into whether a 1-O should have been granted, the defendant must first show that he made every possible attempt to have the SS grant his claim, **including full use** of his appeals rights within the SS.[42] The man who fails to use those rights may not be allowed to argue his objection to the judge, and may end up being convicted even though the local board denied his CO claim illegally.

As discussed in Chapter 16, there is no further appeal from an appeal board if their decision is unanimous. But even if you are turned down unanimously by the appeal board, it still may be possible to avoid induction. The National SS Director has the power to order reconsideration of any classification regardless of the vote of the appeal board.[43] Sending him copies of your CO file and requesting his intervention may be helpful. You may do that on your own, or with assistance from a sympathetic member of Congress.

If you submit substantial new evidence in support of your claim, the local board **must** consider it, and they may be forced to re-open your classification and give you an entire new set of appeal rights.[44]

Some objectors find that there is no relief in sight, and when ordered for induction they decide to refuse to enter the military rather than to violate their conscience. Statistics, for what they are worth, show that objectors who refuse induction after trying **every** other way to get a valid CO claim granted stand about one chance in one thousand of ending up in jail for refusing induction. Of course those statistics don't mean a thing if you are that one guy in a thousand.

The government simply cannot win a court case where a person files a valid CO claim, is determined enough to use up all of his appeal rights attempting to get the claim granted, and then follows through by refusing induction. If anything, his refusal is further proof of his sincere conscientious objection to going into the military. In many such cases the US Attorney (the prosecutor) will review the case, decline prosecution, and send the file back to the local board with a recommendation that they "reconsider" it in light of the new evidence of sincerity--the fact that the man refused induction and risked prosecution rather than violate his beliefs.

Some people have refused induction on the grounds of a denied 1-O claim, and shortly thereafter have received a new classification from their local board. In many cases it has been the 1-O which they requested, but in a few cases it was a new 1-A classification. In either case it means the US Attorney declined prosecution. If the new classification is a 1-A, the objector should be sure to request his personal appearance and appeal rights all over again. (See Chapters 14, 15 and 16.) If you find yourself in this situation, you should have little trouble getting your 1-O granted the second time around, although it has occasionally happened that an objector has had to refuse induction several times before the SS finally understood that he was sincere in his beliefs and was not going into the military.

During past drafts, very few people who refused induction because of a denied CO claim were sent to jail. However, there is always the danger of being charged with violations other than refusing induction. For instance, a person could be in a situation where he could be charged with refusing induction **and** failure to keep the SS informed of a current address, or perhaps late registration. Being charged with two or more counts was used frequently during the Vietnam draft. A conviction on **any** count carries the same five year/$10,000 maximum penalty. People considering refusing induction would be well advised to keep their records clean of all other potential charges, and to have an experienced draft lawyer look over their files prior to the refusal.

For the potential conscientious objector who is convicted in court, an average sentence in the past has been three years of summary probation along with a mandatory two years alternate service work.[45] Since the two run at the same time (concurrently) the whole thing comes out to three years of sending in forms swearing that you have not been caught breaking the law, two years of which must be spent doing alternate service work. But as mentioned earlier, the objector convicted of refusing a **work order** stands a much stronger chance of being sentenced to prison.

The possibility of a prison term, however slim a possibility, along with the fear of being convicted of a felony, seems to scare a lot of people into accepting induction against their judgment. There is an alternative.

An objector who decides not to risk a prison sentence by refusing induction can still have the courts review the SS action on his CO claim by **accepting** induction and having his lawyer file what is known as a Habeas Corpus Petition in federal court. Under that system, the court will review the induction order to see if it was legal, including a review of whether the CO claim was legally turned down. The review generally takes only a week or two, and if the judge agrees that you should not have been drafted, he or she will order the military to **immediately** release you. The problem, of course, is that if the judge feels that the CO claim was properly denied, you are stuck in the military. On the other hand, if you refuse induction you are taking a chance on being convicted and possibly going to jail—particularly if there are other charges that could be brought against you in addition to the charge of refusing induction. Neither alternative is terribly appealing, but at least there are alternatives to choose from. And, for the person who decides to accept induction and whose Habeas Corpus Petition is denied in a court under civil law, there is still the possibility that a counselor or lawyer experienced in **military** law may be able to assist in obtaining a discharge in a military proceeding.

DEPENDENCY DEFERMENTS

If you can show that your induction would cause a hardship to someone who is your dependent, you may be eligible for a dependency deferment (Classification 3-A).[1] Draft regulations say that the term "dependent" means a member of one's close family—wife, child, brother, sister, parent or grandparent.[2] While there are situations where other people, such as uncles, cousins, or "live-in friends" may be dependent upon a draft registrant, the regulations do not allow deferment for men in those situations. Of course, one can always apply and try to convince the local board to bend the rules. But getting them to do so is likely to be rough.

In all claims for 3-A status you must show that your being drafted would cause a hardship for your dependent. Where the dependent is your wife, however, you must show more: you must show that your induction would cause an **extreme** hardship.[3]

There are different kinds of hardship claims: financial hardship, physical hardship, and emotional or psychological hardship. All three are covered by classification 3-A. In the past the most common dependency claim has been based on financial hardship. The form used by the SS reflects the predominance of financial dependency claims in that most of the questions on the form are concerned with money and financial affairs.

Financial dependency

The basis for a financial dependency hardship claim is that your dependent is financially supported by you, and could not get by financially without your income.[4] This is never easy to show, since the SS is looking for cases where, without the applicant's income, the dependent would nearly starve in the streets. By no means does the SS care whether or not your induction would mean that your wife would have to sell the house and move in with her parents. That's quite all right with them, as long as she would have a place to stay and food to eat.

Generally, you must show that if you were drafted, your dependent would have absolutely no one to turn to for help. That doesn't mean that no one is available to help, but that anyone the SS might consider "available" would in fact refuse or not be able to help. For instance, you need not show that your parents cannot afford to support your wife (although that would make a fine claim). It is enough to show that your parents don't like your wife and would **refuse** to assist her financially, even if they had ten million dollars in the bank.

Taking the example a little further, you would also have to show that in addition to having no one to turn to, you and your wife don't have enough in savings or investments for her to get by, that she can not work to support herself, and that even figuring in Welfare and other sources of income, she would not be able to make it. When the SS says extreme hardship, they mean **extreme.** As difficult as it may be to prove all of those things, it has been done successfully by many people, so you shouldn't lose hope.

Because of raises in military pay, military dependency allotments have also been raised. In that way financial dependency claims have become more difficult to prove. Still, considering what the military pays a new draftee, someone who is barely scraping by on civilian wages will probably be able to make out a valid claim for deferment. A person doesn't have to be destitute and in hock up to his ears to qualify. But it helps.

Physical dependency

The second type of hardship claim is that of physical dependency. While this is a rarely claimed deferment, it is probably one of the easiest to get granted, provided that one qualifies for it. In order to qualify, you must be able to show that someone is physically dependent upon you, and that there is no one else who could take your place if you were drafted.

For instance, if Johnny's only blood relative is his mother, and she is crippled and needs him to help her to survive, he may be on his way. Here again we may run into the money game. Considering Mom's Social Security money and any savings she may have, why can't Mom afford to live in a convalescent home? Can she afford a live-in nurse or other hired help to do the tasks which she has relied upon her son to do? The SS isn't going to much care that Mom would prefer to have Johnny around doing them, as long as they feel that someone would take care of her.

Let's look at another situation. Let's say that Paul's living relations are his mother and his retarded brother. His mother can get along by herself all right, but she has to work to support Paul and his brother. While Paul does hold a night job and helps out financially, his real claim may be in the fact that he has to be around during the day to care for his brother while his mother is at work.

Of course, the situations discussed here don't begin to exhaust all of the possibilities. There are some cases where the person claiming physical dependency doesn't even live with his dependent, but still qualifies for the 3-A deferment. The best way to evaluate a situation is to discuss it with a draft counselor. One good rule of thumb is for you to file if you feel that you **might** qualify. The worst that could happen is that the claim will be denied by the local board.

Emotional dependency

The third type of hardship claim is based on emotional dependency. This seems to be a largely over-looked source of deferment, especially for married people and those who come from very close-knit families. In order to get an emotional hardship claim granted, you must show that your dependent is emotionally needful of having you around, and that if you were drafted it would cause the dependent extreme mental anguish and possibly result in psychiatric problems.

Naturally, most potential draftees have family or friends who don't want to see them drafted. But a draft board is unlikely to be sympathetic to a sobbing mother claiming that she couldn't sleep nights if her sweet little darling got drafted. Once again, the key word to remember is not inconvenience, but **hardship.**

A dependent with a past history of psychiatric care makes for a much stronger claim, but that is not absolutely necessary. Nor is it necessary to prove beyond a doubt that a dependent would suffer a complete break-down without you around. The point to make is that it very well could happen, not that it positively would. The important thing is not "proof beyond a reasonable doubt", but enough proof to convince a local board to grant a deferment.

As with a physical hardship claim, you are going to have to work around the traditional Dependency Questionnaire and rely on statements rather than financial resumes to carry the claim. In an emotional hardship claim, a report from a psychiatrist or psychologist concerning the dependent's state of mind is almost mandatory. In cases like that, a sympathetic psychiatrist or psychologist can be extremely helpful.

Filing for a 3-A

The process of filing for a hardship deferment is relatively simple. The claim may be prepared on a Dependency Questionnaire or can simply be documented along those same lines without using the form. The claim may be based upon any of the three kinds of hardship discussed above, or any combination of the three. For instance, if your dependent is both emotionally unstable and depends on your income, both kinds of dependency should be documented for presentation to the board. Let them decide which basis to use for granting the 3-A, but be sure to give them as many realistic options as possible.

In terms of documentation, probably the most important things will be: 1) A statement explaining the nature of the dependency and pointing out why your being drafted will cause a hardship, along with a similar statement from the dependent. 2) If financial dependency is involved, you should work out family budgets that show both the current cash flow situation and how things would change if you were drafted. If you use the SS form, you should be sure not to limit yourself to the tiny spaces provided on the form. 3) You should get statements from others who can verify that the claimed situation exists. This might include doctors, psychiatrists, social workers, ministers, friends, relatives, neighbors, or anyone else familiar with the situation. The letters should be addressed to the local board or "To whom it may concern," but they should be given directly to you and should **not** be sent to the SS. You will want to go over the letters with your counselor before submitting them and will want to make copies for your own files as well.

As with other claims for deferment or exemption, no one will be allowed to submit a claim until after he has been ordered for induction. However, if you think you are qualified for a 3-A deferment you can take advantage of that fact by starting **now** to gather the needed documentation. The claim may require a bit of updating before being submitted at some future date, but at least the majority of the work will be done.

Once a claim has been transmitted to a local board, the board will consider the claim at its next scheduled meeting and decide whether or not to grant the request. Because dependency is a judgmental classification, you have the right to be present at that hearing. If you want to attend the hearing you **must** request a personal appearance in writing before the hearing date has been set.[5] It is best to do this at the same time you submit your claim, or earlier if the opportunity arises. For more information about rights and tactics at a personal appearance, be sure to read Chapters 14, 15, and 16.

If you do not request a personal appearance, or request one but do not attend the hearing, the board will decide your claim on the basis of your written application alone.[6] A personal appearance can make a powerful impression, so the opportunity should be used if at all possible.

Some time after the board hearing you will be notified by mail of the board's decision. If you are notified that your classification is 3-A, it means that the board has accepted your claim and has granted the hardship deferment. Be aware that a 3-A classification is only a deferment, not an exemption. That means that it is not permanent, and that you will need to re-document the claim from time to time, at least once a year.[7] So don't lose track of your draft counselor, your doctor, or others who have assisted you.

On the other hand, you may be notified by the local board that, based on information submitted, they do not feel justified in granting you a 3-A deferment. That does not mean that your claim has been shot down forever, but only that you are going to have to work a bit to try to get it granted. You will have full appeal rights at this point (see Chapters 14, 15, and 16) and should get together with your draft counselor to discuss further action.

There is one other possibility. If the board is convinced that your induction would cause hardship to your dependent, but also feels that the hardship situation is likely to clear up in ninety days or less, it can deny your claim and instead grant you a postponement of induction for up to ninety days.[8] This amounts to a denial of your claim, so you have the right to appeal.

As discussed in Chapter 15, you have the right to present at least three witnesses at your local board hearing. It is strongly recommended that in hardship cases one of your witnesses be your dependent. If a doctor is involved, he or she should also be asked to appear. They are the people best qualified to discuss the claim with the board. In any event, dependency is sometimes difficult to prove to a board, and the help of an experienced draft counselor is highly recommended for anyone considering a 3-A deferment.

SURVIVING SONS

There is a popular misconception that if you are the only male in your family who can carry on the family name you can not be drafted. This just isn't true. The purpose of the surviving son or sole surviving son exemption (4-G) is not to assure perpetuation of the family name, but to limit the number of deaths or disabilities in any one family as a result of service in the United States military.[1]

The 4-G classification actually covers two classes of people: "surviving sons" and "sole surviving sons". Both groups are given a draft exemption,[2] meaning that once you receive a 4-G classification you can never be re-evaluated for the draft. However, if your entitlement to the 4-G should change, or if the availability of a 4-G exemption were eliminated, you could then be subject to the draft.

Neither class of 4-G exemption is easy to get, and the mere fact that such exemptions exist point up the fact that every generation of United States citizens has been forced into war and suffered casualties for nearly the entire history of our country.

Sole surviving son

To qualify for exemption as a sole surviving son one must meet two requirements.[3] First, your father, mother, brother or sister must have been killed in action, died in the line of duty, or died as a result of injuries or disease incurred while serving in a branch of the United States military. Until recently the law did not apply to men whose **mothers** died as a result of military service, but a change to the law in October 1984 has corrected the previous sexist provisions.

The second requirement for a sole surviving son exemption is that you must be the only living son of your father. A man who otherwise qualifies, but whose mother later re-married and had other sons, should still qualify for exemption as a sole surviving son.[4]

Surviving sons

Even if you have living brothers, you may qualify for exemption as a surviving son.[5] To qualify under this class you must show that your father, mother, brother or sister was killed in action or died in the line of duty while serving in the United States military, and that they died after December 31, 1959. You can also qualify if your father, mother, brother or sister died after that date as a result of injuries or disease incurred while in the military. The important thing is the **date of death**, not the dates of service. If your father received injuries during the Korean war, and those injuries caused his death in 1965, you should qualify.

There is also a surviving son deferment (not an exemption) for anyone whose father, mother, brother or sister is presently captured or missing in action as a result of military service.[6] In this situation the 4-G classification would end if the captured or missing family member were to return alive.

General provisions

The 4-G exemption for sole surviving sons and surviving sons will keep you from being drafted into the military or into civilian alternate service work **except** during a Congressionally declared war or national emergency.[7] Bear in mind that **Congress** has not declared a war since 1941 (although the United States has had a couple of undeclared wars since then). Also note that the "national emergency" declared during the Vietnam war was declared by the President, not by Congress, and so the 4-G exemption was still available.

There is no requirement that a man qualified for a 4-G exemption live with or support the surviving family members. If you do, you may also qualify for deferment with a 3-A classification (see Chapter 8). But the Supreme Court has said that the purpose of the 4-G exemption is not only to provide "solace and consolation" to the remaining family members, but also to "avoid extinguishing the male line of a family" by allowing "the death in action of the only surviving son," and to allow "fairness to the registrant who has lost his father" as a result of military service.[8]

One qualified for a 4-G exemption should gather documents to prove it. If you are receiving survivors' benefits, copies of all documents submitted to the Veterans Administration should be obtained. If those are not available, a copy of a death-notification letter or telegram, or a sworn statement from another family member may help. Remember, you need to prove to the SS that a member of your immediate family has died as a result of being in the military.

If the family member died after leaving the military, but death was caused by an illness or injury incurred while in the military, you may run into problems in trying to prove the cause of death, or in trying to document that the illness or injury causing death was incurred during military service. Military medical and personnel records can be obtained under the Freedom of

Information Act from the Military Personnel Records
Center, 9700 Page Boulevard, Saint Louis, MO 63132. A
local veterans' group may also be of assistance. If a
doctor treated the deceased family member for his or her
terminal illness, the doctor may be able to verify the
actual cause of death, and tie it to the military-incurred
disease or injury.

As with all other deferments and exemptions, it
is up to the area office or local draft board to decide
whether an applicant is qualified for a 4-G exemption. If
a claim for exemption is denied, the appeals process
discussed in Chapters 15 and 16 should be used.

MINISTERS
AND MINISTERIAL STUDENTS

The draft law provides complete draft exemption for practicing ministers of religion, with a 4-D exemption.[1] It also provides a student deferment for theological or pre-theological students, with a 2-D deferment.[2] These facts have given rise to a popular misconception that merely being a minister will keep a person from being drafted. Unfortunately it isn't quite that easy.

Ministers

The law exempts both "duly ordained" and "regular" ministers who regularly act as ministers of religion.[3] Apparently the reason for exempting both "duly ordained" and "regular" ministers is to allow the leaders of both formal and informal religious organizations to qualify. In other words, a minister need not be formally ordained to qualify, so long as the ministry is his vocation. But any minister, ordained or not, will qualify for a 4-D exemption only if he is practicing his ministry on a full time or regular basis.[4] This is referred to as the "vocation" requirement.

The vocation requirement for ministerial exemption demands that the ministry must be your chief concern. You must engage in ministerial duties regularly, and be recognized by your congregation as a leader or minister of the group. Merely being ordained, be it by a recognized church or by a group which will "ordain" anyone for five or ten dollars, is not enough.

The vocation requirement does not mean that a minister may not hold a secular job, or work outside his ministry.[5] Most courts reviewing the question have tended to look more toward the importance of a man's activities rather than the amounts of time spent pursuing them, or the formal title given him.[6] However, at least one court has said that local boards may properly consider whether a man spends at least half his time on ministerial duties. The real point seems to be that a 4-D exemption should be given to anyone who is actually acting as a minister. If he must also work at a secular job to support himself or his family, he can still qualify if he shows that the ministry is his main concern and vocation, and that his secular job is secondary to it.

If a minister must hold a secular job because his church, sect or organization can not support him, he should be prepared to submit evidence of that, such as a letter from a superior explaining the situation. If he is taking courses or studying on his own to increase his effectiveness as a minister, proof of that should also be secured. Letters from officers of the denomination or congregation should also be gathered. Those letters should point out his importance to the congregation, as well as emphasizing that he does have a true ministry and a community of faith which he serves.

Difficulties with gaining a 4-D exemption often arise when the ministry is other than "traditional" in nature. Jehovah's Witnesses often encounter problems gaining 4-D exemption, as do "street ministers" or others lacking a well defined "congregation". In such cases it must be shown that the minister serves a community of faith in much the same way a minister with a more tra- ditional congregation serves his community of faith. The real issue here is whether the applicant teaches and preaches the principles of faith and regularly conducts some kind of services for the community to which he is ministering.

The SS may not deny a 4-D exemption to a minister solely on the basis that he has not had sufficient preparation for the ministry or because he has not attended a theological school.[7]

Theology students

Men who attend a theological school and are not yet ministers are entitled to a 2-D student deferment. To qualify for the deferment you must show that you are preparing for the ministry under the direction of a "recognized" church or religious organization, and that you are satisfactorily pursuing a full-time course of instruction in a "recognized" theological or divinity school.[8] A "recognized" theological or divinity school means one with an established reputation, and whose curriculum and academic standards will be acceptable to the church or religious organization sponsoring the student. A "recognized" church or religious organization is defined as one which was established on the basis of a community of faith and belief, and which engages primarily in religious activities. Obviously, if either the school or the church is not well known, and particularly if its practices might not be seen as "religious" by a local board, problems may arise. For instance, courts have said that a group of people who gather together each week to eat peyote buttons and experience nature are not a "church".

A 2-D student deferment is also available to pre-theology students. To qualify you must show that you are preparing for the ministry under the direction of a "recognized" church or religious organization, that you

117

have been pre-enrolled by a "recognized" theological or divinity school, and that you are satisfactorily pursuing a full time course of instruction required for entrance into the theological school in which you are pre-enrolled.

The 2-D lasts only as long as you continue to meet all of the requirements. Should you complete your education and become a minister, you may or may not qualify for exemption as a minister. On the other hand, if you discontinue your course of study, or if the local board feels that your academic progress is not "satisfactory", the deferment could be withdrawn.

"Satisfactory progress" has been defined to mean that during the academic year a man has earned a full proportion of credits toward his degree, enough to complete his degree in the normal time for that program. This means that a student in a four year school must earn **at least** 25% of the credits required for graduation in **each** of his years of study.

A man qualified for a 2-D deferment should gather documents showing his enrollment or pre-enrollment in a school of theology or divinity, and should be prepared to submit proof in support of his claim, such as letters from the school registrar verifying his enrollment, showing his grades, and discussing his rate of progress.

Both the 2-D student deferment and the 4-D ministerial exemption are judgmental classifications, so they will be decided by your local board.[9] You have the right to appear personally at the board meeting to present your case, as well as all the other rights described in Chapters 14, 15, and 16. If you want a personal hearing, you must request it in writing before the hearing date has been set,[10] so it is probably best to make the request at the same time you submit your claim, or earlier if the opportunity arises.

If you do not request a personal appearance, or request one but do not keep the date, the board will decide your claim on the basis of the written documentation alone.[11] The personal appearance can make a very big difference in the board's treatment of a claim, so you should take advantage of this right if at all possible.

MISCELLANEOUS CLASSIFICATIONS

There are six classifications that are not discussed elsewhere in this book. Three are for military members, one is for veterans, one is an administrative classification that you can not request, and the last is unlikely to apply to anyone. In terms of avoiding the draft, this chapter is not likely to be a gold mine.

Being administrative, these classifications will be determined by the SS Area Office. Should the SS Area office deny your claim, you have a right to appeal to a local board[1] where you may choose to personally appear to argue your case, provided that you have made a request for a personal appearance in writing.[2]

Reservists

There are two administrative classifications for military reservists. Class 1-D-D is a deferment for students in college Reserve Officer Training Corps (ROTC) programs, men who have agreed to accept a commission as an officer, aviation cadet applicants who have signed an agreement of service, and most other members of a military reserve unit.[3]

Class 1-D-E is an exemption for students in an approved military college who are enrolled in an officer procurement program, men transferred to a reserve unit after a period of extended active duty, and men who enlisted in a military branch under the Delayed Entry

Program at least ten days before their scheduled induction date.[4]

Active duty military members

Members of the military on active duty are classified 1-C.[5] In most cases the military branch will report your enlistment or induction to the SS, and if your lottery number is reached you will automatically be classified 1-C without ever knowing about it. Also classified 1-C are military aviation cadets, military academy cadets, or those serving with the National Oceanic and Atmospheric Administration or the Public Health Service.

Veterans

If you have completed at least one year of active duty military service, or six years of reserve duty, in a military branch (including the Coast Guard) you are eligible for a Class 4-A exemption from further service.[6] If you have completed at least six months of active duty, and were then either transferred to a reserve component or discharged for the convenience of the government, you also qualify for a 4-A.

Foreign nationals who have completed at least one year of active duty in the armed services of their native land will qualify for a 4-A exemption if their country has a treaty agreement with the US (see Appendix A).

Elected officials

Class 4-B for elected officials is an all-time favorite, because absurdity is amusing and this one is absurd! I can't imagine anyone ever qualifying for a 4-B; they might as well have an exemption for Martians.

Class 4-B is just for you if you happen to be: the Vice-President of the US; the governor or any other elected official of a state, territory, or possession; a member of a legislative body of the US or a state, territory or possession; a federal court judge; a judge of a state, territory, possession, or the District of Columbia.[7]

If any reader knows of a vice president, governor, legislator, or judge young enough to be a member of the Age Twenty Selection Group, please let me know!

On hold

Because all registrants are presumed 1-A, the SS had to figure a way to get around the legal requirement that allows men to submit claims for deferment or exemption whenever they are classified 1-A.[8] They came up with an "administrative holding" classification, Class 1-H.[9] The definition of Class 1-H in the regulations is terribly vague, but it seems to boil down to saying that if you are not currently being processed for induction, you are classified 1-H. Since 1-H is the lowest class of all, there are no appeal rights or processing rights. In fact, you are not even notified that you have been classified 1-H. It is very unclear how you can be presumed 1-A and classified 1-H at the same time, but when dealing with the SS, apparently nothing is impossible.

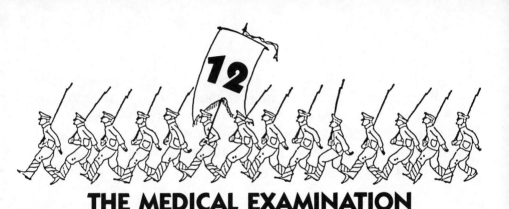

THE MEDICAL EXAMINATION

There are two kinds of classification for people who are considered to be physically, mentally, morally or administratively unfit for military consumption. The classification of 4-F is given to anyone who is permanently disqualified.[1] If someone is found temporarily disqualified, or has a condition which, if persistent, may be disqualifying, he is kept in his original classification (usually 1-A) but is placed into a special sub-class known as RBJ, and can not be drafted until he is given another physical examination and passes it.[2] RBJ means Re-examination Believed Justified.

It should be noted that once a person is classified 4-F he normally will not be re-examined. The 4-F classification is an exemption, meaning that anyone having a 4-F is exempt from the draft. The exceptions to the rule (aren't there **always** exceptions?) are cases where a person is found disqualified and is classified 4-F, but later becomes eligible under a changed or different set of medical standards, such as if he becomes a doctor, if war is declared, or if the physical fitness standards are substantially changed.[3]

The physical fitness standards

The physical fitness standards for induction are set out in Chapter Two of Army Regulation 40-501. The reason they appear in an Army Regulation rather than

Selective Service Regulations is that draft physicals (and enlistment physicals for all branches of the military) are given at the military-run Military Entrance Processing Stations (MEPS). With very rare exceptions, a local board may classify a man 4-F only if he is found to be not qualified for induction by MEPS.[4]

If Congress were to declare a war or a state of national emergency, the medical standards in Chapter 6 of AR 40-501 would be used to evaluate draftees. Far fewer 4-F exemptions would be available under those standards than under the "peacetime" draft standards in Chapter 2. The Chapter 6 wartime standards have not been used since 1945, and it seems unlikely that they will be used again in the future. If and when we see a draft, the odds are overwhelming that it will be a "peacetime" draft such as we had from 1948 to 1973. This book, therefore, only explores the Chapter 2 "peacetime" standards.

The Chapter 2 physical fitness standards are over twenty pages long and contain literally hundreds of disqualifying conditions. The unabridged list is reprinted in Appendix C, but a complete review of all those conditions is beyond the scope of this book. It is important to note that many conditions which are disqualifying might seem almost trivial or even go unnoticed in civilian life. Do not just assume that you are physically fit, because roughly half of the people examined by MEPS over the years have been found not qualified.

The following review of the physical fitness standards does not begin to cover all of the disqualifying conditions listed. It is intended merely to get you thinking about possible eligibility for 4-F.

Abdominal Organs
and Gastrointestinal System

Among the conditions listed are cirrhosis of the liver, hemorrhoids, recent hepatitus, current or recent hernias, intestinal obstructions, megacolon, pancreas diseases, herniated abdominal scars, and ulcers.

Blood System

Anemia, faulty RBC construction (including sicklecell anemia) Hodgkin's disease, and hemophilia, among others.

Ears and Hearing

Damage, disease or defect affecting inner or outer ear, perforation or severe scarring of the ear drum, hearing deficiency or loss.

Endocrine and Metabolic

Diabetes, goiter, gout, hyperinsulinism, beriberi, pellagra and scurvy.

Extremities

Limitation of motion in shoulder, elbow, wrist, hand, fingers, hip, knee, ankle or toes; absence of all or most of a finger or toe; weak or "trick" knees, ankles, shoulders, elbows or wrists; claw toes, flat feet, hammer toes, severe ingrown toenails, arthritis, bone diseases, recurrent dislocated joint, badly healed or presently unhealed fractures.

Eyes and Vision

Numerous eye diseases or injuries are listed, such as chronic conjunctivitis, diplopia, glaucoma, night blindness, vision not correctable to 20/40 in one eye and 20/70 in the other,

20/30 in one eye and 20/100 in the other, or 20/20 in one eye and 20/400 in the other, refractive error greater than +8.00 or -8.00 diopters.

Genitourinary
Absent or nondescended testicle, kidney diseases, albuninuria, bedwetting, amputated penis, prostrate gland hypertrophy.

Heart and Vascular
Organic valvular diseases, heart murmurs, dilated heart, high pulse rate, high or low blood pressure, varicose veins, rheumatic fever in past two years.

Height and Weight
Being too thin or too heavy can be disqualifying. For instance, at 5' 10" a person would have to weigh less than 123 or more than 214. Also, men less than 5' tall or more than 6' 8" are disqualified.

Lungs and Chest Wall
Abscessed lung, acute bronchitis, pleurisy, pnuemonia, recently fractured ribs, sternum, clavicle or scapula; active tuberculosis in past two years, bronchial asthma since age twelve, chronic bronchitis, pleurisy in past two years.

Mouth, Nose, etc.
Allergies, hay fever, asthma (chronic or severe), perforated septum, sinusitis.

Neurological
Degenerative disorders, frequent migraine, tremors, twitches, spasms, etc.

Psychological

Psychosis, neurosis, frequent encounters with police, antisocial attitudes, homosexuality, alcoholism, drug addiction, immaturity, learning defects.

Skin and Cells

Severe acne, dermatitis, eczema, chronic athlete's foot, chronic or severe sweaty palms or feet, extensive or deep scars, plantar warts, skin ulcers, obscene or extensive tattoos, psoriasis.

Spine

Bad backs are difficult to prove, but if verifiable by x-ray or medical history, may be disqualifying.

Miscellaneous

Moderate or severe reaction to bee stings or insect bites, acute deformities, chronic metallic poisoning, frostbite, chilblain, trench foot, predisposition to heatstroke or sunstroke, current or recurring venereal disease.

Documentation

In order to get a 4-F exemption you must have a condition that is considered to be disqualifying, and it usually must appear in the medical fitness standards. However, the MEPS can disqualify **anyone** who in their opinion would not make a good soldier, so any condition which could interfere with marching, jumping, running, standing, and other soldierly activities should be documented.[5]

Let's say you have chronic athlete's foot. (Yes, there are some good ones in the medical fitness standards!) The first big step in any medical claim is to document the condition--get it in writing. Now, whose opinion is the Army going to believe? A doctor, right? So you need to find a doctor who will help you to document your condition for the Army. You can start by asking your family doctor for help with the draft. It is always worth doing, since the worst the doctor can do is to say "no".

There is nothing illegal or unethical about documenting a medical condition. All you want your doctor to do is verify that you have something that is listed in the medical fitness standards. If you have one of the conditions listed you are legally entitled to be found not qualified for military service. It is your right, much like the right to vote or to assemble. And just like those rights, it will be denied to people who don't know the laws or don't insist on their rights.

It has been my experience that many doctors are pro-military, so you may be wasting your time (and

"pseudoeggphobeia: the fear of powdered eggs...

money) with the family doctor, but you never know until you try. It is much better to work with your family doctor if he will cooperate, since he is the one you have been seeing for a number of years. But the really important thing is to have a **strong** doctor's letter, so if the family doctor will not make a commitment to be helpful, you should find another doctor.

In many areas of the country there are sympathetic doctors who will write dandy medical reports for draft registrants, provided the registrant has something worth writing about. Don't expect a "draft doctor" to lie, because he or she won't. But by the same token, a sympathetic doctor can write two pages about athlete's foot, whereas an unsympathetic doctor might write only two lines.

If you are having trouble finding a helpful doctor, you should contact a local draft counselor. If your doctor is sympathetic but not familiar with the medical fitness standards, show him or her Appendix C in the back of this book.

Fees will undoubtedly vary from one doctor to another, and fees will also depend on the services needed. While an office call for a blood pressure test may run just a few dollars, a complete draft physical examination can cost one hundred dollars or more. You should not ignore the possibility of a medical exemption just because you don't have a lot of money. Some doctors will accept monthly payments, and some will adjust their fees according to what you can afford to pay. But, please, please don't rip off a sympathetic doctor, or he may not be available to help the next guy who needs his services.

Once you have found a doctor who will be helpful, you should get the doctor to document your medical condition(s). If you have seen other doctors, you should get those records released to your current doctor. If not, you should explain to your doctor how long you have been aware of the condition and what problems you have had because of it. If you have a recurrent condition, such as athlete's foot, you should get in to see your doctor for treatment every time the condition crops up, and you should make sure that happens fairly often. With a condition such as athlete's foot, you should not just go to the local drug store and buy some foot powder to treat yourself. Sure, it is less expensive that way than going to the doctor, but what are you trying to save, your money or your freedom? A doctor's report is going to be much stronger if it can point to several bad attacks of athlete's foot over a period of months or years. That makes the condition "chronic", as required by the medical fitness standards. You should also remember that your doctor must have something current to document, so you should be sure to have a good case of athlete's foot on the day of your first appointment.

A number of people have regular physical examinations and have been told that they are in good health, so they conclude that they couldn't possibly fail their draft physical. Bear in mind that the purpose of a regular physical exam is to determine whether or not you have a condition that may cause you illness or injury in normal civilian life. A draft physical is given to determine whether or not you have a condition listed in the medical fitness standards.

Many people have conditions that would disqualify them from being drafted and don't even know about them, even though they have a physical exam each year. The fact that you are in good enough health to make the school football team has nothing at all to do with the fact that your athlete's foot is disqualifying. When in doubt, you should have a complete physical examination from a doctor who is familiar with the medical fitness standards.

The way the standards are written, roughly half the people examined at MEPS have been disqualified in the past. No doubt a higher percentage could have been disqualified, if only they had discovered and documented their condition in time.

Whether to see more than one doctor, and whether to see a doctor more than one time, depends upon your condition—both physical and financial. In many cases just one visit to a doctor is enough, as in cases of permanent disabilities. But consider this: the reason for any condition to be disqualifying is that the Army feels that the condition would interfere with your ability to function as a soldier-- either that you would be on sick call all the time, or that the military environment would worsen the condition to the point where you would have to be discharged and possibly given disability payments.

In some cases, such as athlete's foot, a minor attack now and then won't really be a bother. The military can give you a little foot powder and that will be the end of it. On the other hand, if your doctor's report shows that in spite of all the foot powder and ointment prescribed you still can't seem to be without the rot for very long, that is another matter. After all, at home you can change your shoes and socks frequently, wash your feet once or twice a day, and so on. But the military can't guarantee that you will always be able to do all of that, so your condition is probably going to get even worse.

What to do with the report

You should have your doctor release the medical report letter to you. It should not be sent directly to the SS or the MEPS, for two reasons. First, you are going to want to read over the report, and go over it with your draft counselor to make sure that it is a strong letter.

There is no advantage at all to submitting a wishy-washy doctor's letter. In fact, it could be a real detriment to your claim to have a letter in the file which down-plays a condition. Second, you are going to want to run off at least two or three more copies of your doctor's letter—one for your personal file, and at least the original and one copy to take with you to the MEPS physical exam. Remember: get the letter released to you, go over it with your counselor, and make several copies before going any further.

If the doctor's report is written shortly before you take your physical examination, it should suffice. But if the letter was written months previously, you should attempt to get a more recent letter from your doctor covering office visits or developments since the last letter was written.

The physical exam

The pre-induction physical examination will be given on the day you report for induction. As such, it will be a last-ditch affair. If you fail the exam you will be sent home with an RBJ or a 4-F. If you are found acceptable you will be inducted into the military that day and sent off to a basic training camp. Because of this, it is extremely important that you show up for the physical exam with every piece of medical documentation you can gather, and that you do your very best to be found unacceptable. There will be no second chance.

The one possible way to get a second crack at the physical is if you are seeking a 4-F **and** another classification at the same time. In that case you **might** be instructed to report to MEPS as originally ordered, but only for the exam and not for induction.[6] If that happens and you pass the physical, you will be sent back for a hearing on your other claim; you can then appeal the denial of your 4-F claim and agitate for a re-examination.

Let's take a look at a hypothetical pre-induction physical examination. The actual order in which things happen may vary from one MEPS to the next, and may even vary from day to day at each MEPS, but what we are interested in here is not the exact order, but some general guidelines.

One day Phil is ordered to report for induction. It upsets him so badly that he forgets to change his socks for a week, and his athlete's foot crops up again. Poor Phil! He gathers up his doctor's letters about his recurring athlete's foot, and reports to the local MEPS as ordered, at around 7:00 AM.

Immediately upon walking through the door, Phil is assaulted by a screaming maniac who hands him a pile of forms to fill out. At that hour in the morning, who needs this fool? But Phil had better wake up and take a good look at what he is filling out. It could make the difference between passing and failing the physical examination.

One of the forms he has just been handed is the "Report of Medical History." Filling out this form properly can be to his advantage. He should particularly watch for question number eight, asking him to describe his present health. He may be **instructed** to fill in the words "I am in excellent health." But he is not in excellent health. To the contrary, he has a bad case of athlete's foot going for him that day, so he should ignore the instructions. A person may feel good, but still be in poor health. Phil should use the "Report of Medical History" form to explain that he has a case of athlete's foot, that it hurts, that he can barely walk because of it, and so on. The form also asks for a description of past

135

medical history, so once again Phil should tell them all about it. He should make full use of the form. After all, they asked! And he should not forget to mention that he has letters from his doctor with him.

After being allowed "sufficient time" to fill out the forms, which may be quite a while, Phil and his friends will be herded into another room to take the mental test, a form of IQ exam. He shouldn't worry about failing it, since that is nearly impossible to do. If he found the MEPS that morning, he has a good shot at being found mentally capable of being a soldier. Of course, he could fail the test on purpose, but they have him covered on that angle too. There is a regulation which states that if anyone fails the mental exam, his school transcripts will be reviewed in order to determine his mental acceptability. If he got through the eighth grade, he is likely to meet the mental standards. If he graduated from high school, he will automatically be found mentally acceptable. I guess the Army figures that people like that are smart enough to figure out the wrong answers. Awfully considerate of them, isn't it?

After the mental test, which takes forever, the Army personnel will yell at Phil and his friends some more, and then herd them into another room to prepare for the actual physical examination. They will give each man a locker or basket for his clothing, and a cute little green bag to carry his valuables around in. The green bag is as good a place as any for doctors' letters. After all, they are very valuable.

Phil will be instructed to get undressed, except for his shorts, and to put his clothes into the basket or locker. It has been the experience of some people that the Army is embarrassed by nude bodies, and that anyone who forgets to wear shorts to his physical examination is told to go back and put his pants on, rather than run around nude. This creates quite a scene, so don't forget to wear shorts to your MEPS physical.

At the beginning of the physical, Phil may be instructed to hand in any doctor's letters which he has. If so, he should hand in one set, and keep the other set in his hot little hand (or his hot little green bag.)

Next, he will be herded through one station after another where examiners will weigh and measure him, give him an eye test (they count them--people with one to three eyes pass the test), a chest x-ray, instruct him to leak into a bottle (this is not a co-ordination test), take a blood sample, and check his blood pressure. At any of the stations where Phil thinks that he should fail, he should not take any guff from the examiner. He should explain to the examiner why he feels he should be disqualified, and not let up until he is disqualified. If the examiner refuses to disqualify him, Phil should jot down the station number and the examiner's name and move on.

Most of the people Phil sees at MEPS are **not** doctors. Almost all of them are military medics who know how to take x-rays, collect blood samples, weigh people, and so on, but have little or no medical training.

Eventually our friend Phil will come to a point where there are several doctors sitting behind desks interviewing people. It is usually best to pick the slowest line, since the faster a line moves, the less time that doctor is spending on each person. If Phil has not yet handed in his doctor's letters, or if he has handed them in but for some reason they aren't in his file (they do sometimes get "lost"), he should hand a set to the doctor now. He should be sure that the doctor reads his letters and considers them carefully. He should make the doctor examine him, and insist that he be disqualified. If someone at one of the previous stations refused to

137

disqualify him, he should point that out to the doctor, and point out why that examiner was wrong. Phil should be especially sure to show the doctor his toes and tell him all about the problems of recurrent athlete's foot, and how he just can't seem to get rid of the disease. In short, he should do everything in his power to be found unacceptable.

Before leaving the doctor, Phil should ask him if he will be disqualified. If the doctor says that he is finding Phil acceptable, Phil should ask him why. He might explain to the doctor that chronic athlete's foot is disqualifying under Chapter Two, Section XVII, of Army Regulation 40-501, subsection 2-35(h), and that unless the doctor finds Phil unacceptable he is breaking the law and violating his rights.

If the doctor is still unconvinced, Phil should ask to see the officer in charge of the MEPS. In one successful case, a fellow jotted down the doctor's name and station number, then informed the doctor that he had a disqualifying condition, that he had a doctor's letter verifying that condition, and that unless he was found unacceptable he planned to sue the doctor for malpractice. He was immediately sent to the officer in charge, who found him unacceptable. Doctors are more and more terrified by the words "sue" and "malpractice," especially when used in the same sentence. If all else fails, one can go all the way to the top and demand to see the commanding officer of the MEPS. If even he is no help, get his name as it may be needed later.

When Phil is finished with the interviewing doctor, he may be required to go through the rest of the physical examination even if he has been found unacceptable. If Phil has a letter from his psychiatrist he will be given a short interview with an MEPS psychiatrist. Once again, he may encounter difficulty in being found unacceptable for induction, and should not allow himself to be brushed off or pushed around.

About the only fun things left are the mobility and flexion tests. Everyone takes off their shorts and stands in a circle. The examiners will have people do push-ups, jump up and down, do deep knee bends, and so on. If a man is claiming a bad knee, shoulder, back or such, he **must** avoid doing anything which might strain his weak or bad body part. The examiners will undoubtedly yell at anyone refusing to follow instructions, but if a man goes ahead and successfully performs a motion which causes him pain or strain, he will likely be found acceptable regardless of his doctor's letters.

For example, one man had a shoulder that dislocated almost any time he put more than normal strain on it. At his physical, the examining doctor read his letters, then instructed the man to do one push-up. He did it. The doctor looked at him, looked at his doctor's letter, and found the guy acceptable. After all, his shoulder hadn't dislocated.

At the final check-out station you should be told whether or not you have passed the physical exam. If you have been found acceptable for induction, you will then be herded into yet another room (after being allowed to dress) where you will be inducted into the military. Immediately after the induction ceremony you will be an official member of the military, and will be ordered to get on a bus headed for a basic training camp. If you refuse that order, you will be subject to a military court-martial trial.

If you have been found unacceptable, either temporarily or permanently, you will be informed of it. Be sure to find out whether your disqualification is temporary or permanent. You will then be allowed to go home. If you have been found permanently disqualified you should shortly thereafter be re-classified 4-F.

Re-examination

If you are found unacceptable, this doesn't automatically mean that you will be classified 4-F. A large number of the conditions listed in the medical standards, such as high blood pressure, underweight and overweight, hemorrhoids, broken bones, and so on, are considered to be temporarily disqualifying conditions. It is therefore completely possible for you to fail your physical examination but not be re-classified 4-F because the Army feels that re-examination at a later date is justified. If that occurs you will keep your classification (1-A, 1-A-O or 1-O) but will be placed in the special "hold" category, RBJ. People in the RBJ category cannot be drafted until they pass a re-examination.

At some later date, perhaps a few weeks, perhaps as long as a year, you will be called back to MEPS for a physical re-examination. If you fail the second examination for the **same** reason that you failed the first examination you should be found permanently disqualified and re-classified 4-F. But if you fail the re-examination for a **new** reason (such as if you were disqualified at the first physical because of a broken arm, then fail the second physical for another temporary condition, such as blood pressure) you can be re-called for further examination. If you fail the second physical examination for a permanent reason, such as having flat feet, you will not be re-examined. Lastly, should you be found acceptable at the second examination, you may be inducted into the military that day.

Some unusual cases

Some people have found that they have no disqualifying conditions, but have devised ways of appearing to have conditions which would make them unacceptable. The following examples are given only to show how the pressures of the draft can cause you to be dishonest. I certainly don't encourage anyone to do any of these things, as they are highly illegal, and some are downright unhealthy.

One young man had his room-mate, a medical student, put a plaster cast on his arm the evening before his scheduled induction. Naturally the people at MEPS took it on good faith that the fellow had a broken arm, and they sent him home with a temporary disqualification. Such a practice is called conspiracy to evade the draft, and could get you into a lot of trouble if you were to get caught at it.

Some people have impregnated a cigarette with India Ink, then smoked it. Apparently the ink stains the smoker's lungs and appears in an x-ray to be tuberculosis. This could be very dangerous to one's health.

There have been stories about people putting "additives" in their urine samples. One fellow found out that albumin in the urine is disqualifying, so he stuck some dried egg (very high in albumin) under his fingernails, then deposited it in his urine sample. Unfortunately for him the examiners immediately realized that if he really had that much albumin in his urine, he would be very ill, if not dead. He was prosecuted for providing false information in an attempt to gain an exemption from the draft. Another person tried the same thing, but put in so little albumin that it went unnoticed at the physical examination.

A very popular thing to do at one time was to conceal a pin in the lining of one's shorts, prick a finger with it, and squeeze a few drops of blood into the urine. It was thought that this would appear to be a kidney infection. However, kidney infections are characterized by the presence of dead blood cells in the urine, not live ones. Furthermore, very few people realized that if one truly has a kidney infection the bladder is usually quite sensitive, and failed to respond properly when prodded by the doctors.

Another very popular "trick" has been to use drugs, especially amphetamines, to give a person high blood pressure. Since most MEPS doctors are aware of such tactics, it is usually difficult to fool them. The old stand-bys of using coffee or caffeine tablets, not sleeping for a day or two, or smoking lots of cigarettes, have been used quite a bit, but are usually ineffective unless a person's blood pressure normally runs a bit high. In cases of blood pressure, the MEPS will often insist on morning and afternoon blood pressure tests for three consecutive days, so any artificial stimulation of one's blood pressure would have to be effective for a prolonged period of time.

People have been known to strap coins tightly to their arms or legs for several days before a physical exam, causing what appear to be external ulcers. Some people have applied chemical irritants to their skin, or in some other way caused themselves to come down with a case of skin rash or dermatitis.

There is also a story about a fellow who pretended to be hard of hearing. He was tested several times, and each time responded only to the loudest sounds. When the examiners were done testing him they pointed him toward an open door and indicated that he could leave. As he walked out he was softly instructed to close the door behind him. Without thinking, he reached for the door knob, and passed his hearing test.

A common occurence many musicians have noticed is that after playing for a while, especially in a loud electric band, one can't hear properly for several hours. There have been people who spent the night before their physical examination playing music or listening to their stereo loudly through a set of headphones. They turned the volume up as loud as they could stand it and played hour after hour of loud music, numbing their ears. As a result, they couldn't hear properly for hours. Many failed the hearing test at the MEPS. However, it should be noted that there is scientific proof that loud music can cause a permanent hearing loss. In one experiment, several rats were totally deafened for life after exposure to persistent loud music. So, don't let your pet rat turn up the volume too much—it could make him go deaf.

One last example is sickening to relate. One man drank no liquids for twenty-four hours before his induction physical exam. Then, just before leaving the house in the morning he drank down an entire quart of vinegar. When it came time for the MEPS to test his urine it was almost pure acid, and they were unable to test it. The examiners knew that he had done something, but they couldn't figure out just what it was that he had done, so they sent him home with a temporary disqualification. I would imagine that he was probably sick for a day or two afterwards. He was a sick civilian, but he soon had to face another examination.

You may have heard stories about people shooting off toes or fingers, getting obscene tattoos, or otherwise mutilating their bodies to stay out of the draft. That sort of thing will usually work, but if anyone is so desperate to avoid the draft that he would seriously consider a life-long mutilation of his body, he should first exhaust every other possible avenue. I suggest going to a sympathetic psychiatrist and documenting the emotional problems he is experiencing.

It is true that psychiatrists are not inexpensive. A good psychiatrist may cost hundreds of dollars by the time you are through. But, after all, how much money is a toe or finger worth? More than that, how much money is peace of mind worth?

Generally a person is better off to consult a psychiatrist rather than a psychologist, or an orthopedist rather than a chiropractor, since the MEPS gives more weight to letters from medical doctors.

Conclusion

All things considered, there is no reason for anyone to be drafted who doesn't want to be drafted. Under current medical fitness standards, it is fact that roughly fifty percent of the people examined by MEPS have been found unacceptable for induction. With knowledge of the medical fitness standards and proper medical documentation, no doubt even more people would qualify for the 4-F exemption.

GAYS AND THE DRAFT

If you are gay, dealing with the SS can be easier in some ways and more difficult in others. For some gays, sexuality never enters the draft picture; for others it is the major issue.

First, the big question: what is "gay"? For at least the past forty years it has been clinically recognized that human sexuality is not easily subject to labeling; people do not fit well into neatly defined pigeon-holes. The number of American males who have never engaged in same-gender sex represents a distinct minority. Yes, that is right; less than half the population is exclusively either "gay" or "straight" throughout their lives.

When dealing with the SS, an "either/or" definition of sexual orientation will apply: either you are straight, or you are gay. For example, someone that is actually bisexual will be considered to be gay. Despite the fact that both the American Psychiatric Association and the American Psychological Association have long ago agreed that homosexuality is not a mental disease or defect,[1] the Army Regulations still list homosexuality as a "psychosocial condition" under the section on mental disorders.[2]

It is interesting to wonder how anyone would be drafted if the regulations were literally and strictly enforced, since over half of all men might have to be

145

given a 4-F exemption for homosexuality. The answer is that the regulations are not literally and strictly enforced; many men do not consider themselves gay even though they meet the military definition, many others simply choose not to raise the issue, and some men get drafted despite being gay and saying so.

Until the late sixties a man would almost automatically get a 4-F exemption simply by claiming homosexuality. Word quickly got around, with the result that thousands of men who didn't want to be drafted started claiming to be gay. It wasn't long before the psychiatrists at MEPS refused to believe such claims, and, as a result, many gay men were found to be qualified for induction. In at least one disturbing case, a MEPS psychiatrist felt "he didn't look like one!" When the man refused induction, he was charged and convicted of refusing induction despite ample proof at trial of his homosexuality. The conviction was upheld by an appeal court.[3]

Whether to use being gay as a way to get a 4-F exemption is a hotly debated issue in the gay community. Some people feel that "coming out to get out" reinforces the military notions that gays are defective people. Others argue that if the military insists on creating a way out for men who are attracted to other men, why not use it? Many of the other classifications in this book may apply to you: you may be a conscientious objector, physically disqualified, a ministerial student, and so on. As with any other decision about the draft, only you can decide what strategy is best for you.

Registration

The law requires draft-age men to register regardless of whether they would ultimately be qualified for induction. Courts have said that being qualified for a 4-F exemption does not affect the registration requirement and is not a defense to a charge of nonregistration.[4] For that reason, gay men of draft age are required by law to register. Proof of homosexuality is not a defense to a charge of nonregistration.

The decision of whether or not to comply with the registration requirement is, of course, personal. You may share some of the reasons to register that straight men have: patriotism, belief in following the law, fear of prosecution, the need to qualify for student loans or other federal benefits, and so on. However, barring a complete reversal of military policies concerning gays, you can register knowing there is little likelihood of ever being inducted.

Gay men may also share some of the reasons of conscience or politics that cause straight men not to register. However, you should bear in mind that being ordered for induction can subject you to unpleasant choices that straight men do not have to face: the choice between concealing your gayness and risking harassment or punitive discharge from the military, or admitting homosexuality and being forced to "come out" in situations and times not of your own choosing.

If you are considering draft resistance, you should be aware that imprisonment can be especially serious for gay men. Although it is unlikely that draft resisters will do a long stretch in federal prisons, and although federal prisons are generally better run than most state prisons, even so, you should consider the possibility of prison violence that is frequently directed against gays. A prison experience can be extremely difficult even without such extra abuse.

Documenting your claim

Having to "prove" to MEPS that you are gay can seem amusing, but it is a serious matter when you have to do it. If you claim to be gay, you will probably be referred to a MEPS psychiatrist for an interview (remember, they think you are mentally disturbed). Technically this is to determine whether or not you have a "mental disorder" or "psychosexual condition" of homosexuality.[5] More likely the interviewer will have some vague ideas about determining whether or not you are a homosexual; since homosexuality is not an illness, a doctor can no more diagnose "a case of homosexuality" than "a case of tallness," but that is their problem. In the past the examining psychiatrists have approached this task in different ways. Freudians might ask you to talk about your mother, while behaviorists might ask about the decor of local gay bars. I mentioned above the psychiatrist who decided that the man being drafted "didn't look like one." These are the people who think **you** are crazy.

Opinions differ on whether or not to use documentary evidence of being gay. If you have read the rest of this book you know I think it is important to document **any** claim, and it should be done whenever possible. Since it may be difficult or impossible to appeal a MEPS determination, it is safest to do everything possible to convince the MEPS psychiatrist that your claim is true--and to build up evidence that can be used in court if it comes to that.

The most effective documentary evidence is probably a report from a psychiatrist. It need not document "a case of homosexuality," but might, for instance, indicate that you were treated for emotional stress caused by coming out, family tension over being gay, or the break-up of a relationship with another man.

Letters from other doctors might also be helpful. For instance, your doctor may be able to write a report showing that you have requested VD testing which straight men are unlikely to request (rectal cultures), or that you have requested AIDS screening, or that a case of hepatitis or VD was attributed to gay sex.

Although MEPS strongly prefers letters from doctors, you may want to consider letters from friends or family. MEPS personnel will often believe that you might lie to get a 4-F, but it would be harder for them to believe that family and friends would all join in a false story. Of course most people have no "proof" of your homosexuality, so can only report their opinion. Be **sure** to read the cautions below before providing anything more specific.

If you have ever been in legal trouble involving homosexuality, such as indecent exposure, solicitation, and so on, your arrest and court records could provide evidence that you are gay, and may also be separate ground for a 4-F on "moral" grounds.

Some cautions

If you claim to be gay, the examiners at MEPS may try to interrogate you about specific names, dates, places, acts, and so on. They may even say that without that information you can not be given a 4-F. **That is not true!** Proof of specifics is not necessary, and it could land you and others in a mess if you give it.

In many states same-sex relations are still illegal. In those states it could be dangerous to use your gayness at MEPS, especially if you give any details about your sex life. You might be confessing to a crime. Even if same-sex acts are legal in your state, that quickie in the bushes at the park could land you in jail if you tell MEPS about it. Be very careful, and if at all possible clear everything with your counselor or lawyer before telling MEPS about it.

You should know ahead of time how much you are going to tell MEPS and where the line is drawn. Be prepared to defend that line. You must be able to give them enough information to show that you qualify for a 4-F, but not so much that you end up in trouble. If MEPS wants more than you and your counselors are prepared to give them, try informing MEPS that your lawyer told you not to say anything more. That usually works.

I strongly advise against providing MEPS with explicit photographs or written statements or anything else that could be called pornographic. Not only to you run the risk of having such evidence used against you, you may also run afoul of laws that make possession, transfer, or mailing of pornographic material illegal.

Privacy of records

Information that you give to MEPS or the SS is supposed to be kept confidential.[6] However, information about criminal acts can be turned over to police. There are other loopholes, and the law is sometimes broken. Some employers may want to delve into those records, especially if your job requires a bond or a security clearance. Employers can not **legally** have access to the SS records without your permission, but if they ask for your permission, you are in a bind. If you give permission and the employer is homophobic, you may lose your job or promotion. On the other hand, if you refuse permission, it will almost certainly cost you the job or promotion. The best solution is not to work for homophobes, but that is not always possible.

Discrimination

You could possibly encounter SS or MEPS personnel who harass or insult you for being gay. Such conduct seems less likely these days than ten or twenty years ago, but it could happen. If it does happen, try to get the names of the people involved, including witnesses, and report the incident to their superiors. You may also want to discuss the incident with a friendly lawyer, a sympathetic member of Congress, or a local gay rights group.

Unfortunately it seems almost inevitable that some homophobic incidents will occur. Accepting that as reality does not mean that it should be tolerated. To the contrary, it means that any board members or other personnel of MEPS or the SS who exhibit such behavior should be educated—or if necessary intimidated—until they clean up their act.

PART THREE: THE END GAMES

APPEALS
AND
COURT

HOW TO DEAL WITH
A DISAGREEABLE CLASSIFICATION

If you are classified and feel that you should be given a different classification, you have the right to present that claim. The only time this isn't true is when you are in the no-man's land of Class 1-H. If you present a claim for a judgmental classification, it will be ruled on by your local board.[1] Claims for administrative classifications will be ruled on by the SS Area Office.[2] In either event, if you don't get the classification you want, you have the right to appeal.[3] You also have the right to appeal if the Area Office denies your request for a student postponement.[4]

Procedures differ slightly depending on what kind of claim you make, but in all cases your induction will be postponed while you are using your appeal rights.[5]

Student postponements

With the exception of the student postponement, most other postponement requests carry no right of appeal. Once the Area Office grants or denies your request, that is the end of the official line. Even so, it may be possible to have your Congressional representative intervene on your behalf. Given the very short deadlines involved, it would have to be done almost immediately.

Denial of a student postponement request by the Area Office can be appealed to the local board.[6] To that extent it is the same as appealing a denied administrative classification, so the procedures below apply. The big difference is that if the local board also denies the request there is no further right of appeal.[7]

Administrative classifications

If you are seeking an administrative classification (1-C, 1-D-D, 1-D-E, 4-A, 4-B, 4-C, 4-F, 4-G, 4-T, or 4-W) your claim will be reviewed by the Area Office.[8] A claim for Class 4-F will almost certainly be denied unless MEPS reports that you have been found unqualified[9] (see Chapters 12 and 13 for more about 4-F). If the Area Office does not grant your claim, you can appeal that decision to the local board.[10] If the local board also turns you down, you can appeal to the District Appeal Board,[11] and again to the National Appeal Board if the District Appeal Board turned you down with a split vote.[12]

Judgmental classifications

Claims for classes 1-A-O, 1-O, 2-D, 3-A, and 4-D are judgmental classifications and as such are considered first by the local board.[13] If you are claiming conscientious objector status (1-A-O or 1-O) you **must** appear at the local board hearing.[14] If your claim is for classes 2-D, 3-A, or 4-D, you may choose whether or not to appear.[15] If your claim for a judgmental classification is denied by the local board you can appeal to the District Appeal Board.[16] If denied again by a split vote, you can appeal to the National Appeal Board.[17]

Why you should appeal

Some draft registrants wonder why they should bother to appeal. They seem to feel they are likely to be inducted eventually, so why prolong things?

156

It may very well be that you will eventually be inducted, but here are two facts for you to think about:

* More than 180,000 men avoided the draft in early 1972, and they had one thing in common: they had all stalled off their induction, either by appealing or by other methods.

* Most changes in classification come about as a direct result of a local board personal appearance.

Even if your classification is not changed as a result of appealing, you are no worse off. In fact, you are probably much better off in four important ways: First, you have let the SS know that you are not happy about the classification you have been given. Second, you can not be inducted while you are in the appeal process. Third, you have submitted evidence to show why you should have a different classification, you have built up a file, and this can make a **very** big difference in the eventual outcome of your case. Fourth, you have forced the draft board to take some kind of legal action, which means they have to justify not changing your classification. This gives the SS more chances to screw up something, and believe me, they are a bureaucracy, and they are good at screwing things up. It happens very often. Such mistakes, known as "procedural errors," can make a great difference in your processing.

I believe that one should almost always appeal any classification they don't want.

How to appeal

The most important part of the appeal process is to pay very close attention to deadlines. The regulations say that if you do not request something before the deadline runs out, you have given up your right to request it.[18] If you do not file for an appeal before the deadline, you've given it up. If you do not request a personal

157

appearance within the set time, you can't have one. The system plays for keeps and excuses are rarely listened to.

You are allowed only fifteen days from the **mailing date** of the notice of denial of your claim in which to request an appeal.[19] Considering that mail may take several days to be delivered, you can see the urgent need to be completely prepared and in touch with your mailbox.

If you wish to appear personally when the District Appeal Board hears your appeal, you must say so in your letter requesting the appeal. If you do not ask for a personal appearance, the claim will be decided in a closed session.[20] Conscientious objectors are **not** scheduled for a personal appearance at the Appeal Board unless they have specifically requested one in writing, the same as every other claimant.

For example, if your classification request was denied by your local board on August 1 and notice was mailed to you on August 3, you have until August 18 to request an appeal. If the Area Office denied your request for an administrative classification or student postponement on August 1 and mailed you a notice on August 3, you have until August 18 to request review by the local board. In either case, your request does not have to be in the hands of the SS by that date, but it must be postmarked no later than August 18.

Your request should be in writing, in the form of a letter or on the form provided. It should contain your name clearly typed or printed, the date, your Selective Service number and your signature. If you send a letter it can be lengthy or short. About all you need to say is, "I appeal." This is also the best time to add, "I request a personal appearance."

Communicating with the SS

This is a good time to bring up a few points about communications with the SS. I have already mentioned the importance of keeping a copy of your registration form, and having proof that you registered on time. Any further communications with the SS, including any changes of address, should **always** be in writing and should be sent by **certified mail, return receipt requested.** You should also keep at least one photocopy of **everything** that you send the SS, and should keep **everything** that they send to you.

No, I don't work for the Post Office or own a lot of Xerox stock. There are some good, practical reasons for these suggestions, as illustrated in the examples below.

Let's say that Steve Huston files a 3-A claim and goes down to his Area Office to request a personal appearance. What proof does he have of having requested it? None! Even if he presents his request in writing, what if the clerk "loses" his request? What if, two weeks later, the clerk denies ever having seen Steve? Steve is in trouble!

If Steve had sent his request by **certified mail, return receipt requested,** he would have legal proof of who at the SS office received it. If he also kept a photocopy of his request, he would have legal proof of just what it was that he had mailed. Without that proof, he may be denied the right to a local board personal appearance.

Let's take another example. Let's say that Chuck Liebling got a very low lottery number and is ordered to report for induction. Along with the order for induction he also receives a questionnaire asking, among other things, whether he is a conscientious objector. Chuck immediately fills out the form to indicate that he is a conscientious objector and mails it off to the SS. However, somewhere between his local post office and the SS office, the letter is lost.

A few weeks pass, and Chuck begins to wonder what has become of his request to be classified as a conscientious objector. He contacts his Area Office, and is told that no such request was ever received, that he failed to report for induction as ordered, and that his file has been turned over to the United States Attorney's office for prosecution. If Chuck had used certified mail, return receipt requested, and kept a copy of the form, his lawyer would have no trouble getting the charges dropped and forcing Chuck's local board to hear his conscientious objector claim. As it is, Chuck may very well be prosecuted, convicted, and sent to prison.

Certified mail, return receipt requested, involves the use of two Post Office forms. The first, the certification receipt, is date-stamped at the Post Office at the time of mailing. It provides proof of the date of mailing, and also shows the address to which the letter was mailed. It should be immediately clipped or stapled to the photocopy of the letter and put somewhere safe, where it won't get lost or eaten by your kid brother. The return receipt is a little card which you address to yourself. It is attached to the letter that you are mailing, and the certification number is recorded on it. When the postal person delivers the letter, the addressee (the SS) has to sign for the letter. The return receipt is then removed from the letter, date stamped, and mailed back to the sender. It is your legal proof that the SS got the letter, when it was received, and who received it. The return receipt should be attached to the photocopy of the letter and kept in your file.

In order to send mail certified, return receipt, it is necessary to get window service at the Post Office. Be sure to bear this in mind when calculating deadlines. For example, if you are requesting an appeal and your fifteenth day falls on a weekend, you will have to mail your request the previous Friday. If you wait until Monday, it will be too late.

The law regarding a registrant's communications with the SS is very bad. You are legally responsible for receiving all mail sent to you by the SS, and you are also legally responsible for all of your mail getting to the SS. Apparently the SS just isn't very responsible. There is no real way to insure that everything the SS sends out will get delivered, other than to keep the SS informed of a current mailing address. But there is a way to have proof concerning everything that you send to the SS, so you

should make use of it. You should send everything by certified mail, return receipt requested.

The reason for keeping photocopies may not be clear yet. One of these days it just may happen that you will need to have legal proof of something that you sent to the SS. For example, Steve Huston needed proof that he requested a personal appearance, and Chuck Liebling needed proof that he claimed to be a conscientious objector.

Even people who do not find themselves in such serious circumstances may have many uses for photocopies of the letters they have sent the SS. For example, it is always very helpful to bring a complete copy of your SS file any time you see your draft counselor. Getting a copy of the file from the SS is not impossible, but it is often a giant pain in the rear. Once you finally succeed in convincing the clerk that the law gives you an absolute right to obtain copies of the contents of your file[22] (which may take quite a bit of persuasion) you will be charged twenty-five cents or more per page for copies.[23] A hand-written copy is not legally binding—it has to be a photocopy or a carbon copy.

If you happen to own a portable photocopy machine, the SS **may** let you use it to copy your file. Then again, they may not. Of course, you can always take your file to a copy machine to make copies. But the SS has the strange notion that if they let everyone borrow their SS files a few of them might not come back, so they send a local board clerk along with men who check out their files. All you have to do is to set up an appointment well in advance, and pay the SS an hourly rate for the services of their clerk.

The bottom line is that it is much easier, faster and cheaper to make at least one clean photocopy **before** sending anything to the SS, and to save all letters you receive from them. Most libraries have photocopy machines that cost only five to twenty cents per page. Once you have a photocopy made, you should not let go of it—you should always have at least one copy on hand.

You may have noticed that my attitude toward the SS is not trustful. There is good reason for this. Ever heard of the Peter Principle? According to Dr. Peter, people rise to their level of incompetence. As long as a person can handle a job, he continues to be promoted, until promoted to a job that he is incapable of doing. Even though a person may be the best clerk in the office, he may not be up to being a vice-president. In that case, once promoted to vice-president, he will not be recommended for further promotions. Unfortunately, no one will recommend him for a demotion, either. So there he sits for the rest of his life, screwing up a job he can't handle.

The SS is a prime example of the Peter Principle in action, since it is a government bureaucracy. Most local board members have no idea what the SS regulations say; they accept the word of the clerks who are government employees. Most clerks are merely clerks, and no more. If they know anything at all about the SS law, they usually interpret it incorrectly. But that doesn't stop them from answering questions from board members or from registrants. To the contrary, they are more than happy to inform the local board members that it is all right to deny a conscientious objector claim on the ground that a man is not a Quaker, and they are tickled to tell a registrant that he might as well not bother appealing, since he will just get drafted anyway.

This is why I keep stressing that you should not trust these people with your future—unless you don't care about your future.

THE LOCAL BOARD
PERSONAL APPEARANCE

A local board will hear your claim for any of the judgmental classifications (1-A-0, 1-O, 2-D, 3-A, and 4-D). It will also hear appeals from a denial by the Area Office of your request for any other classification or a denial by them of your request for a student postponement.

Any time your claim is being reviewed by a local board you have the right to attend in person and present your case.[1] The right to a personal appearance is extremely valuable and you should make full use of it, even if it means some inconvenience or sacrifice.

If you are seeking conscientious objector status, you will automatically be scheduled for a personal appearance with the local board.[2] If you are requesting any other judgmental classification, or appealing an Area Office denial of an administrative classification or a student postponement request, you must ask for a personal appearance when you file your claim or appeal.[3] The most important point to remember is that you **must** request a personal appearance within the time set by the SS, otherwise you lose the right (see Chapter 14).

This chapter and the next one will assume that you have exercised your right to have a personal appearance and have sent a written request within the time required. Once received by the SS, you will be mailed a notice of the date, time, and place for your personal appearance. That notice **must** be mailed at least ten days before the meeting date.

Why appeal?

The kinds of tactics you will want to use at your personal appearance depend upon what your current classification is and what you want to do about it. If you are appealing only as a stall tactic but don't really feel that you are qualified for any other classification, then your tactics will be very different than if you are seriously set upon winning some specific classification, such as conscientious objector status.

One thing should be brought up here. A lot of people may want to appeal their classification because they think they should be classified 4-F. You should be aware that in most cases the local board will not give you a 4-F exemption unless instructed to do so by the MEPS.[6] In other words, you **must** fail an MEPS physical examination before being eligible for a 4-F exemption. Generally speaking, you are not going to get a 4-F exemption as a result of a personal appearance. However, you should go ahead with it anyway. It is certainly better than not appealing at all, and it may do you some good by focusing attention on your medical claim. If nothing else, appealing will protect you from an induction order while you work something out medically.

A tactic that has been used by some people is to appeal just for the sake of appealing. Let's say that you have an induction order, but have no reason to feel qualified for any classification other than 1-A. Obviously, you are unlikely to get any other classification simply by appealing. But then again, you won't get inducted while appealing, and that is worth something. It is up to the

SS, not you, to decide whether you qualify as a CO, minister, or whatever else you may claim. Even though it may not really get you anywhere to appeal, it could still be worth doing.

Some people feel that there is little use in stalling off induction by appealing. They feel that stalling the draft is just putting off the inevitable, and that they will eventually be inducted anyway. There are four points they should consider. First, every day that you stall brings you closer to the magic age of twenty-six when you will no longer be draftable. Second, using appeal rights even as a stall forces the SS to take some kind of action, and gives them an opportunity to commit procedural errors which could result in a benefit to you. Third, it just may be that while appealing you will realize that you are a conscientious objector, or may develop or discover some basis for 4-F exemption or some other deferment or exemption. Last, approximately 180,000 men escaped the draft in March, 1972, with only one thing in common--they had all been stalling. None of those people would have been around to escape the draft if they had not been stalling, some for as long as five years.

If you are appealing as a stall tactic, you might get a kick out of reading sections of the Nuremburg trials to the local board. Or you might want to read them the parts of the United States Constitution which prohibit slavery and indentured servitude. Or maybe just sing the National Anthem and walk out. Another idea is to read the Ten Commandments and then ask the board members why they are drafting people even though a person should not kill and should not covet his neighbor's goods. The board members will likely get embarrassed and terribly defensive in the face of such questions. With a little creative thought, most registrants should be able to come up with all kinds of inspiring ideas. Just a couple words of caution: it is illegal to intentionally disrupt local board business,[7] so you should be sure that you are very clear on how your information affects your draft status. Also, harassment tactics are unlikely to endear you to the local board members, and this should be considered if you may ever request some deferment or exemption from the same local board.

If there is a particular classification you qualify for, it is not recommended that you get too strange with your local board. They just aren't likely to grant your conscientious objector claim if they recall seeing you a few months before under embarrassing circumstances.

Assignment to a local board

When you register you are asked to provide a "permanent address." If that address changes, you are supposed to notify the SS of your new address within ten days.[8] When you file a claim that requires action by a local board, you will automatically be assigned to the local board for the area containing the address you gave the SS.[9] If your residence is not the same as your permanent address, such as if you gave your parents' address in Montana but you are living and going to school in Seattle, you can be reassigned to a Seattle local board. To do that you must request the change, in writing, at the time you file your claim.[10] If you change your address after the claim is filed, you can still request reassignment so long as the local board has not yet acted on your claim.[11] In any event, you are only entitled to one reassignment until after your claim has been decided.[12]

Think about it. You get to choose the local board that will hear your claim, because the "permanent address" you give them is completely in your power. As long as mail will reach you quickly and certainly at that address, regardless of whether you live there or not, you are legal.[13] If you find out ahead of time that the board covering the address you gave is the pits, you get another shot at it by requesting a transfer. This is powerful!

Choosing a different board could make all the difference in the world to your life. During the Vietnam draft we found shocking differences in the way claims were handled by various local boards. For example, some boards did not give out a single 1-O classification in five years, while another board a few miles away granted more than half of the 1-O claims it heard.

Granted that no draft board is great, the fact remains that some are far worse than others. As a general rule of thumb: rural boards are less likely to grant claims than urban boards, and boards covering conservative communities are less likely to grant claims than boards in more liberal areas. Naturally, there are exceptions, and it may well be that a rural board would be more sensitive to a dependency situation than some urban board. There won't be any definitive answer until the local boards start establishing their track records. See a local draft counselor for the latest info.

There are obvious practical considerations involved. It makes no sense to get assigned to a local board that is hundreds of miles away and where you have no close contacts. You need to receive mail sent to you, meet deadlines, review your file, make your personal appearance, and otherwise have ready access to the local board. But if you can do all that, and if you still have a choice between a fair board and a bad one, then go for it!

Witnesses

You have the right to present witnesses at your personal appearance,[14] and it is strongly recommended you do so. The decision of the local board will be based upon the information in your file at the time of the personal appearance and any new information presented at the time of the personal appearance.[15] Presenting witnesses is a very good way to submit new information, especially if you are requesting conscientious objector or hardship status.

The purpose of presenting witnesses is to let the board hear first-hand information from people who know your situation quite well from their own observation and experience. You are entitled to present up to three witnesses, but the local board can agree to hear from more than three if it wants to. However, local board members tend to be not very nice, so you shouldn't count on having more than three witnesses heard, or any other favors. If you feel that your case would be best presented by using more than three witnesses, you should go ahead and ask the board if it will agree to it. It is always worth a try, but you should be prepared to have your request turned down. Decide ahead of time which three witnesses are most important to your case.

Time is precious. The local board may cut off an appearance after only ten or fifteen minutes, and that is barely enough time to clear your throat unless you and your witnesses are **very** well prepared. If your three witnesses take only three minutes each, that leaves you only one to six minutes to present your claim. The board could conceivably give you lots of time, but the law does not provide any guaranteed time limits, so be prepared to move quickly in case you are strictly limited to ten minutes or less.

Advisors

For the first time ever, SS regulations in 1982 created a new right: the right to have access to an advisor.[16] This is not quite the same as being represented by counsel, but it is the right to have your counselor or lawyer with you and to consult with him or her during the hearing. The board can exclude your advisor from the hearing only if he or she is disrupting or unduly delaying the hearing.[17]

Your advisor is not a witness. He cannot address the board or answer questions for you. For tactical reasons you are not going to want to consult your advisor constantly, since that may give the board the impression that your claim is an invention of the advisor's imagination. Even so, it will no doubt be a big help to have your advisor there for moral support, to remind you of things you are forgetting to cover, to help you spot any trick questions that may come up, and to consult with if you don't know what to do next. You advisor may also be able to help out with some of the paperwork discussed below.

Other rights

If you do not speak fluent English you have the right to bring an interpreter to the hearing.[18] Since the hearing is a very important event, you might want to have an interpreter with you to be sure you and the board always understand each other.

There is a limited right to have the hearing open to the public.[19] In most cases the hearing will be closed—the only people present will be board members, a clerk, you and your witnesses and your advisor. However, you have the right to ask that the hearing be open to the public, and that request should be granted unless the board has a good reason to deny it. The board chairperson has the right to exclude the public or to limit the number of people attending a hearing only if it becomes disruptive or disorderly.

Some guidelines

The exact strategy and tactics you will use depends entirely upon your individual situation. This is something you and your counselor can best work out. However, several pointers are offered here which can be useful at almost every local board personal appearance where you are requesting a change of classification. Realize that these are just general practices and not a substitute for competent draft counseling.

Above all, you must stay sober. Yes, sure, you can function better stoned than you can when not stoned, but if you go to your local board appearance all blitzed out, the board will walk all over you. With cleats on. They will chew you up and spit you out, and it will take you a week to figure out what happened. They just aren't very mellow people, and you have to be alert and attentive.

You should write up a brief summary of the points you want to make at your personal appearance. It doesn't have to be very long—a page or two is fine, and more than that may be too much. It should be typed, or at least hand-written very neatly and legibly. You should make about six copies. It is fine to use carbon paper for the copies, but the copy you keep in your personal file should be a photocopy. Here's another reminder about your personal file: you should keep everything the SS sends you, and at least one photocopy of everything you submit to the SS. (Be sure to read "Communicating With The SS" in the previous chapter).

Along with your summary, you should outline your main points on an index card, an old envelope, or have them tattooed on your arm. You only need the original copy of these notes.

If at all possible, you should try to find at least one person who can go to the draft board with you as a witness to testify in your behalf. You should ask your witnesses to write up summaries of the points they want to make, and get six copies made for the hearing plus one for your personal file. Witnesses should make notes of their main points, just like you did. Last, but certainly not least, you should make the necessary arrangements with your draft counselor if you intend to have him there as your advisor. You will probably also want to have your counselor look over your written statement and those from your witnesses to make sure that everything is in order.

Playing draft board

A week or so before your personal appearance you may want to get together with several friends, or better yet several draft counselors, and play draft board. It isn't as much fun as playing doctor, but it can help you to get your thoughts together for the actual personal appearance. This process has been found to be very helpful for people who are trying to obtain conscientious objector status, although it is helpful for anyone seeking any deferment or exemption. It often happens that a local board will catch a person unprepared and use the personal appearance to confuse hell out of him. After fifteen minutes of stuttering and stammering, trying to come up with rational answers to irrational questions, you won't appear too convincing to the local board. They will feel that they are justified in denying the claim, since you couldn't even answer "simple" questions.

Playing draft board can get you well enough prepared to stand up under the local board's games, no matter what they try to pull. It could also help you to prepare yourself for some of the draft board's ridiculous questions, such as "What would you do if someone were raping your mother?" or "What would you do if God told you to fight a war?" Most draft counselors will have a list of the kinds of questions that draft boards have asked conscientious objector applicants in the past. Those questions may appear senseless, but should be considered. After all, someone else had to deal with being asked those questions, and your local board may enjoy asking them again.

At the personal appearance

By the day of your local board personal appearance you should be well prepared. You should not plan anything for the rest of the day, because you are going to be quite busy.

It is best to show up a bit early for a personal appearance. You will most likely have to wait quite a while before you get in, but if you show up late the board may refuse to see you at all. Take a good book or your knitting. Perhaps a rousing game of pinochle between you and your witnesses might pass the time.

Eventually, you will be called into the local board meeting room. Make sure to glance at a watch or clock and jot down the time of day on the back of your notes. You should bring your summary of important points with you, and have your witnesses bring theirs (all six copies of each). If you have more than three witnesses, you should have copies of their summaries as well. The summaries should **not** be turned in before meeting with the board members. You should keep them in your hot little hand until needed.

The law requires that a majority of the board's members be present.[20] Since a board must have at least three members, and most have up to five, you will be heard by between two and five people.

If you have more than three witnesses you should explain your situation to the board chairperson and ask if the witnesses can testify. Explain why it is necessary to present all of them. You might also want to throw in something about how difficult it was for them to attend the hearing, but that they were willing to do so because they know how important the matter is.

When witnesses are admitted, they should read or paraphrase their summaries, and then hand each board member a copy of the summary, explaining that the summary was written by themselves, not you. The witnesses should also be prepared to field any questions which the board members throw out. In selecting witnesses, you should choose only those people able to accurately represent your position, and who will be familiar with your circumstances. Make sure your witnesses know they have only a few minutes to speak.

If any (or all) of your witnesses are not going to be admitted, you should **tell** the board that you are going to read the statement(s) prepared by the witness(es). You should not ask them, you should **tell** them. Then, before they can say yes, no, or maybe, you should start reading. When you are done reading, or when the local board cuts you off, you should hand each board member a copy of the summary. The original should be handed to the chairperson of the board with a request that it be included in your file. By law, it **must** be.[21]

You now have the attention of each board member. The paper you have just given them is probably the only piece of evidence they have touched all day. Suddenly, the board members are interested. They have been made to feel important, because now they have something to do besides just sitting and listening.

Next, you should start in on your own statement. The procedure is the same here as for the witnesses. Keep in mind that timing is very important. DO NOT hand the board members their copies until you have read or paraphrased your statement. That way, you will probably get to make your points clear to the board. If the copies were handed in before giving testimony, you might be told that the board members will read them later. That could be a mistake, not only because the board might not read the statements at all, but also because it would destroy the impact necessary for getting the individual board members involved and interested. Get the picture? Make your point first, then give them something they can read and ask questions about.

Another important technique is to try to have the testimony of witnesses given before yours. Should time run out after you have testified, but before your witnesses have finished, the board can cut off further discussion by demanding that the witnesses either hand in their written statements or not, as they please. But if the board feels time has run out before you have testified, it would probably be illegal for them to terminate the hearing without allowing you to testify.

If you get interrupted in the middle of a point, or if for any reason you feel that you haven't gotten your point across (board members are not always swift on the uptake) you should use your notes to remind you of the points you need to make. You should not be afraid to make the same point more than once. Sometimes it is the only way to get through.

The board members may bombard you with questions. If so, you should try your best to answer them clearly and in as **few** words as possible. It is best to keep answers short and to the point, since the questions may come down in a rapid-fire attempt to confuse you. If given time, you should go ahead and expand your answer, but you should try to make your point in the first few words. That way, even if the answer is cut short, you have already said what you need to say.

When answering questions from the board members, it is good to keep in mind exactly what you are there to talk about. Don't let the board side-track you. If you are there to talk about your opposition to all war in any form, the differences between Buddhism and Catholicism don't make a damn bit of sense as a topic for discussion.

Above all else, you should keep cool. No matter what happens, do not lose your temper. If necessary, stop and take a deep breath. Call them all a bunch of bastards, but **silently.** For your own sake, you should **not** tell board members where to go. It is in your own best interest to stay calm and remain courteous. If any board member treats you unfairly, seems biased, shows prejudice, or somehow shows that he or she is not familiar with the contents of your file, you should make a note to yourself about it. Get the board member's name, if possible, because it may come in handy later.

Another tactic the board may use is to sit there looking very uninterested and ask you what you want, or hit you with a statement like, "You are the third guy we have seen today who claims to be a conscientious objector. We turned down the others. What makes you different?" If that happens, you should take over the meeting. You should read your statement, have your witnesses present their testimony, tell the board everything you can think of that relates to why you should have your classification changed, and encourage the board members to ask questions. If they give you the ball, run with it!

If you have an advisor with you, his main job may be to sit there and look decorative. Naturally, you may want to consult with him if you have questions, and he may want to prod you if he feels you are missing the point of the question or straying from the important points in your claim. Your advisor could also help by keeping track of time, date, names of board members present, and so on.

But remember that your adviser is not allowed to address the board or answer questions for you.[22] It is also possible that frequent consultations with your advisor could hurt your claim by making it appear that you are unable to answer the questions, and that you have to get answers from your advisor. It could cast you in a bad light. If there are hostile members on the board, they could force your advisor to leave the hearing if they think he is feeding you answers or delaying the proceedings through frequent or prolonged consultations.[23] None of this means that you should be afraid to consult your advisor; don't hesitate to do so if you need help. But try not to over-do it.

At the end of the interview you should ask the board members if anything is unclear, or if there is any reason why they feel you do not qualify for the classification you are requesting. If one or more of your witnesses were not allowed to testify, you might ask the board if it will consider hearing from that witness now. When all is said and done, you should thank the board members for their time and leave the room.

On the way out, glance at a clock or watch and jot down the time, but do not leave the building yet. You should wait until the next person is called into the hearing room, and again record the time.

More paperwork

Next, walk out into the lobby and have a seat. This is where the real work starts. You should immediately write down as much as you can remember about what went on during the hearing. It doesn't have to be in order or exact wording, but you should get down everything you can recall. To begin with, stick to what actually went on, since that is what you will forget first. Note your comments and reactions later. If you feel that you were mistreated, make a note of how and by whom. If there were any questions you were not allowed to answer fully, note it and write out a full answer. Don't pretend that you answered completely at the appearance. Rather, you should play up the fact that the board did not allow you to answer fully. A typical entry might read, "Mr. Jones asked what I would do if someone raped my mother. I answered that I could not say, since the situation had never come up. I was about to add that under no circumstances would I kill the man when I was interrupted by Mr. Smith."

If there was any inference that board members were not familiar with your file, you should be sure to include that in your summary. For instance, "Mr. Smith asked if I were aware that I could have filed as a conscientious objector at an earlier time. I had to point out to him that I had done so. It seems that Mr. Smith was not at all familiar with my file."

If you feel that any or all of the board members treated you poorly, or didn't pay attention, discriminated against you in any way, or just generally bad-mouthed you, you should note it in your summary. If you feel that any of the questions asked were unfair or irrelevant, you should note it and explain why.

The reason for writing up a summary of the board meeting is that no actual transcript of the hearing is made.[24] Unless you put together your own summation of what occurred at the board meeting, the only record will be whatever the board members or the clerk writes up for inclusion in your file.[25]

You may be wondering why you were instructed to jot down the time of day on three separate occasions. Believe it or not, there is a method to this madness. If you know what time you went in to the hearing, and what time the meeting ended, and what time the next man was called in, you can compute two very important bits of information. You will know how long the meeting lasted, which could be important if you feel you were not allowed enough time.

You will also be able to compute the time from the moment you walked out of the hearing room until the next man was called in. Since the board votes immediately after hearing each case, you will know how much time the board spent discussing and voting on your claim. That information should also go into your summary.

While you are busily writing up your summary of the hearing, there are a couple of things your witnesses can be doing. If they were allowed in to testify, they should compose their own separate summaries of the meeting. If everyone was called in together, you may want to help each other recall the details of the meeting and write up one group statement that everyone signs.

If for some reason any witness was not admitted to testify, that witness should write a letter to the local board expressing disappointment at not being allowed to testify. The letter might stress what an inconvenience it was to take all that time and trouble, just to be turned away. It might also say that unless the board felt it already had enough evidence to grant the requested classification, it was very arbitrary of them not to consider all of the available evidence in support of the claim.

When you have finished writing up your notes, take them home with you. Go over them later and see if you have anything to add. You may want to put things in chronological order. Put a statement at the end saying something like, "Unless I am notified otherwise, I will assume that the local board accepts my summary of the hearing as complete and accurate." Type up a clean final version and make copies of it for your file. Also gather up photocopies of the summaries written by your witnesses and save them in your file. All summaries should be sent in by certified mail, return receipt requested.

Your summary and those of your witnesses should be dated, and should have your name and SS number on each page. The summaries should be mailed to the local board within a week of the personal appearance date. If you wait any longer than a week to submit a summary it may not carry as much weight.

Notification of results

You should be notified of the results within a couple of weeks after the hearing. If you were turned down by the board, there are many things to be done. You will have fifteen days after notice of the denial was sent in which to request an appeal.[26] You have the right to a personal appearance before the District Appeal Board, and to have an advisor present, just as at the local board appearance.[27] However, you do not have the right to present witnesses at the appeal board level.[28]

As with the local board hearing, it is strongly recommended that you take advantage of all your rights. Even if you for some reason do not want a personal appearance with the appeal board, you may still request that your file be sent to that board for review.[30]

Going about a local board personal appearance properly is a lot of work. As I keep saying, the SS just isn't very nice. If you want a classification other than 1-A you are going to have to work for it, but you can succeed if you are willing to put in the time and effort required.

All of the paperwork that you prepare and submit after your local board personal appearance can be used to your advantage at the district appeal. With a good case and a little bit of luck the appeal board will reverse the decision of the local board and grant the classification you requested.

THE DISTRICT APPEAL
AND BEYOND

Shortly after your local board personal appearance you will be notified of the decision of the board. If your claim was granted, your notification will show that you have been given the classification you requested. If your claim was denied, you get the news.

If you are denied by the local board, all is not lost. You have fifteen days from the date the notice is sent in which to request an appeal to the district appeal board.[1] At that time you may also request the right to appear in person before the district appeal board when it considers your case.[2] If you appear, you may have an advisor with you, but you may not present witnesses.[3] You can submit any new evidence, written or oral, such as letters, documents, or your own presentation.[4] As with the local board personal appearance, it is suggested that you make full use of all your appeal rights. If you do not want to make a personal appearance, you still have the right to have the appeal board review your file and any new information that you submit when you request an appeal.[5]

Checking the file

There are several things you should do before requesting an appeal. The first is to tie up all the loose ends from your local board personal appearance. If you have not yet done so, you should make sure that your summary of the local board personal appearance, along with the statements of your witnesses and any other related paperwork, have been submitted to your file.

The next step is to find out why the local board denied your claim. The local board is required to give reasons for turning down a claim.[6] If reasons for denial were not sent along with the denial of your claim, it would probably be quickest and easiest for you to go down to your area office and ask to see your file. If you are not able to do that yourself, you can request the board's reasons by mail, or you can authorize some other person to review your file. If possible, you should check your own file, since you know best what information you are looking for.

The board's reasons for denial should be included as a part of the local board summary. There should also be a record of how the board members voted on your classification. That information may be useful, so you should get a copy of it. If possible, you should try to find out how each individual on the board voted. It is best for you to have photocopies of these documents, so you should ask the clerk at the area office to make copies on their machine. There will be a charge for that service, but there shouldn't be more than two or three pages.

While checking out your file you might as well make sure that your summary of the personal appearance and the statements of your witnesses are in the file. If they aren't, you should provide the clerk with duplicate copies of them. You may also want to include copies of the mail receipts proving that you mailed the summaries to them, along with a letter explaining that you are providing duplicate copies of the paperwork which they seem to have lost. You might be rather upset about such carelessness and may wish to say so in your letter.

If for any reason the documents that were submitted at the personal appearance are not in your file, duplicate copies should immediately be submitted, along with a letter requesting a full explanation of where the originals have gone, and also asking whether the board members considered the documents when deciding to deny your claim.

If you go in to check your file and find that it is not in the area office, you should immediately demand to find out just what has been done with it. Demand to see the head clerk. Chances are that if the file is not in the area office at this point it has probably been sent to the district appeal board prematurely. That has been known to happen in cases where the local board is careless or trying to push a person through without giving him a fair chance. It is illegal to send your file off unless you have requested an appeal, or unless (very rare) an appeal has been ordered on the initiative of the National Director of the SS. Tell the head clerk that sending your file out is illegal, that you want it back and that they are not allowed to send it out without your written request.

Anyone in this situation should also get off a letter or phone call to the State SS Director. Your draft counselor will have the address and phone number. In your communication with the State Director, you should explain that you have just found out about your file being prematurely sent to the appeal board, and ask the State Director for his personal attention to the matter. You should let the State Director know when your local board personal appearance was held, what the mailing date is on your latest classification notice, and that you have not yet requested an appeal. You should explain further that you have more information to submit to your file before the appeal, and ask that your file be returned to the area office immediately, **before** being reviewed by the appeal board. If the communication with the State Director is by telephone, you should send a letter (certified, return receipt, of course) confirming the phone conversation, including any promises made by the State Director.

If you really want to do a job of it, you can also request that you be sent written notice when the area office receives your file back, and that you be given a fifteen day period from the date of the written notice in which to prepare your file and send your request for an appeal to the appeal board. You should be sure to indicate your name and SS number in all communications, and you might want to send your letter to the State Director by Special Delivery, as well as certified, return receipt.

In one case where a man had to send a letter to the State Director about his file being sent off prematurely, he received a very apologetic reply two days later, and all of his requests, including the request for an extension of time to appeal, were granted.

You should find out why your claim was denied by the local board. When the board classified you they were required by law to review everything in your Selective Service file. In truth, they probably didn't, but that is another story. At any rate, if you presented a claim for deferment or exemption the board must have reviewed the claim. If the claim was denied, the board is **required** to give reasons **in writing** for the denial.[7] It may be that those reasons were sent to you along with your classification. If not, you can request them by mail, or you can go to your area office, ask to see your file, and get a copy of the reasons. If no reasons have been given, you should definitely demand them, pointing out that this procedural error on the part of the board is prejudicial to your rights. That should scare hell out of the clerk, and get you some written reasons in a hurry.

Once you know why the local board denied your claim, you should do your best to show why those reasons are not valid. There are two ways to do this—legally and factually. The board can't turn down a claim just because it doesn't like you or doesn't agree with you. The reasons for turning a claim down must be legal. For instance, a board can not turn down a CO claim because a man has long hair, or a purple mohawk, or doesn't belong to a church. Turning a man down because of the length or color of his hair is called "personal prejudice," and is not a legal thing for a local board to do.[8] Also, there is no legal requirement that a conscientious objector must belong to a church. In fact, the SS regulations specifically state that a conscientious objector does not have to believe in a God, let alone belong to a church.[9] So that kind of reason is illegal as well.

Factually incorrect reasons are the ones that are not supported by the information in your file. Let's say that the board turns down your conscientious objector application because they feel you are "insincere" in your beliefs (a very common reason given in conscientious objector cases). First, the board must show exactly what information in the your file leads them to disbelieve your sincerity. If the board cannot show where it got the information causing it to disbelieve your sincerity, the reason is probably invalid. The courts have repeatedly held that mere disbelief is not reason enough to deny a conscientious objector claim.[10]

If the local board can show a reason for denial ("registrant insincere based on evidence of membership in rifle club"), your job in the appeal will be to show why the board's conclusion is wrong ("although I belong to a rifle club for target shooting, I would never kill a living thing, since living things are a part of God. I certainly would not participate in war in any form.")

187

Once you know why the board turned down your claim, it would be a good idea for you to discuss their reasons with your draft counselor. Your counselor will be able to tell you whether or not a reason is legal, and will probably have some suggestions on how to best go about showing that the board reached an incorrect conclusion.

Preparing the file

Using the information gathered from the file, you should write up a statement explaining why you feel that the local board was wrong in not changing your classification. It may be that the board's reasons for denial were incorrect, that the reasons were not legal, that you feel the board failed to consider all of the available information, or any number of things. The point is: you know the board should have changed your classification, but it didn't, so it must have done something wrong. Your job is to make a good case for what that something was, and make it so clear that no one can fail to see it.

You may also want to have your draft counselor check your file to see if he or she can find any errors or illegalities. If so, you should be sure to point them out to the appeal board in writing.

If you feel that you were treated improperly at the personal appearance, you should say so. Point out exactly how, when, and by whom. You can use examples from your summary, the local board's summary, or anything else in the file to prove your points. If need be, you can also gather additional evidence to support your claim and add that to the file too.

You may be wondering if all this paperwork is really necessary. I feel that it is. Whether or not you have a personal appearance with the appeal board, you are going to want to have a file that is strong enough to support your claim in the face of a local board denial.

What is in the file? First, the evidence that you submitted before and during the personal appearance. Next, the local board's reasons for finding that information insufficient. If you leave it at that, you will lose the appeal. The district appeal board would simply uphold the local board's decision. So you submit your summary and the statements of your witnesses. Now you are even-up with the local board again. But you want to tip the scales in your favor, so you submit your statement explaining all the things you feel the local board did wrong. Now the appeal board will have only one of two choices. It can grant the classification you want, or it can come up with totally new reasons for denial.

There is a great deal of truth to the rumor that appeal boards tend to rubber-stamp the decisions of local boards. One big reason for this is that people in the past either didn't know how to prepare their file for a district appeal, or just didn't bother to do enough work. Those who have decided to live within the system, damnable as it may be, might as well know how to get what they want from it. The draft will not go away if ignored. The man who wants a deferment or exemption is going to have to want it badly enough to work for it.

The appeal

Within the fifteen day deadline, you must write a letter requesting that your file be sent to the district appeal board. It is best if you have prepared your file by this time. If you want to appear personally before the appeal board, you must also request that in your letter. The request for an appeal **must** be postmarked not later than the fifteenth day after the mailing date on your latest classification notice, and should of course be sent by certified mail, return receipt requested.[11] The request should include your name, the date, your signature, and your SS number. A copy should be kept for your personal file.

If you are requesting a personal appearance with the appeal board, you must be given at least ten days' notice of the date when the appeal board meeting will be held.[12] Your presentation at the appeal board meeting should be along the same lines as at the local board personal appearance, with the exception that you will not be allowed to present witnesses at the appeal board. You should be prepared to discuss your situation with the appeal board, and to point out to the appeal board members why you feel that the local board's decision was wrong.

After the appeal board personal appearance you should prepare a summary of the meeting, just as you did after the local board meeting. Once again, you should take it home, clean it up, and submit it to your **area office** within a week of your meeting with the appeal board.

If you asked for a personal appearance before the appeal board, but for some reason you were unable to attend the meeting, you should immediately submit a written statement explaining why. If you submit your reason quickly, and if the appeal board feels that it is a good reason, it can decide to reschedule your appearance,[13] but it doesn't necessarily have to. If there is no time when you can expect to be able to meet with the appeal board, you should explain that to the board and request that it review your file.

After a district appeal you will be notified of the appeal board's decision by mail.[14] Your next move will depend upon just what the notice says. If the appeal board grants the classification you want, that may be the end of it.

If denied again

If your claim was denied by the appeal board, you should check the notice carefully. It should show the vote of the appeal board. If you are denied by a split vote (such as 2-1) at the appeal board, you have the right to appeal the decision to the national appeal board.[15] You will again have fifteen days in which to request the national appeal. Prepare it just the same as you did for the state appeal, making note of the reasons for denial given by both the local board and the state appeal board. If you are entitled to a national appeal, you also have the right to a personal appearance before the national appeal board.[16] Your letter requesting a national appeal can follow the same guidelines as your letter requesting the state appeal, and should be sent to your **area office.**

In most cases the vote of the state appeal board will be unanimous. If that is the case, you have no further right to appeal. If you are classified 1-A or 1-A-O, you can be ordered for induction immediately. A man in the same situation but classified 1-O can be processed for alternate service work. Some local boards in the past made it a practice to send people in this situation an induction order within a few days of the classification notice from the appeal board, and some boards even sent the classification notice and a new induction date in the same envelope. It saves postage.

There are several steps that can be taken even if the appeal board turns you down unanimously, although there is no guarantee that they will work. Anyone facing induction doesn't really have much to lose by trying them, and with a little luck you might get a national appeal granted.

192

In cases of denied conscientious objector claims, the National Inter-Religious Service Board for Conscientious Objectors (NISBCO), or the Central Committee for Conscientious Objectors (CCCO) may be able to persuade the national board to consider your file. Those organizations will need a copy of your file to work with, along with power of attorney to act on your behalf, so you should be sure to send those things. Their addresses are listed in Appendix B.

If you can come up with new evidence to submit in support of your claim, or if the reasons given by the state appeal board are not legal reasons for denial, it may be that you can get your case reopened. Many conscientious objectors have found it helpful to write their local board a letter expressing their concern over the fact that their current 1-A status from the appeal board means that they are going to be forced to refuse induction if ordered, since the SS didn't seem to understand that they are sincere in their beliefs. In the hope that the SS won't make them break the law, they ask their local board to reconsider their classification. Don't do this unless you have thought it out very carefully and you **really** mean it!

Forced reopening is also a possibility, and can be very effective for people who need the time afforded by a double appeal process. Let's say that Jack Randolph is currently classified 1-A and about to have his district appeal board hearing where he plans to pursue a 3-A hardship deferment. The day before his appeal board appointment Jack turns in a conscientious objector claim to his area office. Since he has never before filed as a conscientious objector, and because the information he submits, if true, would warrant a change in his classification (from 1-A to 1-O), his local board must consider his claim unless the state appeal board grants him a 3-A deferment.[17]

Let's say the hardship claim is denied by the appeal board with a unanimous vote. Shortly after his meeting with the appeal board, Jack should receive a notice scheduling him for a new personal appearance. (Remember, a personal appearance is **automatically** scheduled in CO cases.) If the local board denies his CO claim, he can appeal that decision.

What course of action you should take after your appeal is a matter that can best be decided by you and your draft counselor. There are a number of possible tactics, some discussed here and some not. The "best" thing to do will depend on two things—your classification, and what you hope to accomplish.

DRAFT CASES IN COURT

During the Vietnam era there was so much publicity given to draft cases in court, especially Supreme Court decisions, that many people began to think that going to court was one of the steps in appealing an unsatisfactory draft situation. The Selective Service Act makes it very clear that in most cases this cannot be done.[1] While it is possible to get a court injunction against the SS under certain conditions, and in rare cases it is even possible to have a federal court review your classification, the most common way to "take a case to court" is to be the defendant--to have the United States government bring charges for an alleged violation of the Selective Service law.

The usual charge landing people in court has been refusing induction, although people have also been taken to court for refusing to register, late registration, destroying draft board files, trashing draft boards, and so on. Since refusing induction is the most common charge, that is the one we will focus on in this chapter. (See Chapter 3 for a discussion of current registration cases.)

We should first take a moment to consider what it means to be a defendant in court. If it were possible to sue the SS, a person could bring suit any time he was displeased with his draft situation. If he lost in court, he would be no worse off than he was before the suit. Congress realized that, and realized what it meant in terms of bogging down the system and the courts. That is why the Selective Service Act is designed to prohibit suits against the SS.

As a defendant, you stand to lose a lot if your court case fails. In order to get to court, you first have to violate the law. Any violation of SS law carries a maximum penalty of five years in prison and/or a ten thousand dollar fine.[2] Taking a case to court is not a simple matter of filing suit against the SS. To get into court you have to bet up to five years of your life that you will win. I am a gambler, but at those stakes I am not about to bet unless I am pretty sure I have a winner.

Going to court almost always complicates a case, especially since the prosecutor may decide to charge you with every possible violation he can dig out of your file. For example, it may be that a man will be charged with refusing induction, and also with failure to register on time (because he registered two months late) and with failure to keep the system informed of a current address (because he moved and didn't tell them for a month). It is possible to be acquitted on the charge of refusing induction, but still be convicted on other charges. Because of the possibility of multiple charges being brought, it is usually best for you to try very hard to clear things up through the SS before it gets to the point of going to court. Usually a bit of effort, along with the attitude that you sincerely want to straighten things out through the system, will be enough to get what you want from the SS. Of course, there are times when no amount of effort seems to work, and a confrontation in court is the best or only choice you may have.

If you are going to end up in court, you probably will stand a much better chance of winning if you have a good draft lawyer handling your case. The court may offer free lawyers if you can't afford a private lawyer. In some courts a man may be allowed to choose the lawyer he wants to represent him, but in most cases getting a free, court-appointed lawyer means that you will have to accept whomever the court appoints. That is fine until you discover that the lawyer you have been given has never handled a draft case, right? In one case, a court-appointed lawyer actually talked his client into accepting induction rather than going into court, even though the man had a good defense, because the appointed lawyer did not know enough about draft law to spot the defense.

If you don't know a good draft lawyer, your draft counselor may be able to recommend someone. You might contact the local chapter of the National Lawyers Guild or the American Civil Liberties Union for referral to a draft law specialist. In many cases those groups can help you find an experienced draft lawyer even if you have but little money to pay.

There are three main lines of defense used in cases of refusing induction: (1) procedural errors, (2) ungranted classifications, and (3) challenging the constitutionality of the draft. There are pros and cons to each kind of defense, and many times more than one approach will be used in the same defense.

Procedural errors

Probably the most common defense used is that of procedural errors. Any time the SS takes action in processing a person toward induction, there are certain legal guidelines which must be followed. The processing procedures are defined in the Selective Service regulations and in the Registrant Information Management System Manual. These two documents are very lengthy and make boring reading, but they may be helpful to anyone who thinks he may have spotted a procedural error.

Any time the SS fails to follow the correct processing procedure, the system has violated your rights under SS law, and has committed a procedural error. In cases where a procedural error has no bearing on your present draft situation, it is probably not useful as a defense. The courts usually hold that a procedural error must be prejudicial in order to give rise to a defense. But in many cases an error will have some bearing on the case and will be deemed to have prejudiced you. Since it takes many steps to process you for induction, especially if you requested some deferment or exemption, the SS has many opportunities to commit errors, and very often one error leads to another. Cases involving procedural errors seldom get as far as a full trial, although they may go to trial if there is a question of whether the action of the SS was legal, or whether an illegal act was prejudicial.

As an example of a procedural error which would raise a valid defense to a charge of refusing induction, let's say Jimmy Sarni submits a valid claim for conscientious objector status. The local board denies the claim and immediately orders him to report for induction. The order is illegal, since Jimmy must be allowed time in which to exercise his appeal rights. If Jimmy reports as ordered and refuses induction, the procedural error will act as a defense to the charge. However, it will not be a defense to some other unrelated charge, such as late registration.

Well before trial the United States Attorney's office reviews draft files to decide whether or not to pursue the case. If one or more prejudicial procedural errors are found, or if your lawyer contacts the US Attorney and points out procedural errors, the file may be sent back to the area office along with a letter explaining that the government chooses not to prosecute. The SS must then re-process you, starting from the point of the earliest procedural error. In many cases that means that the local board will reconsider your classification, with the right to a personal appearance and an appeal. Every once in a while when the SS has really botched a case, files have been known to mysteriously disappear.

Ungranted classification

The second type of defense involves an ungranted classification, or what is known as a "basis in fact" defense. There are times when a person feels that he is entitled to a certain classification, but for some reason the SS refuses to grant it to him. This is especially common with conscientious objector classifications, although it has happened with other classifications as well. After going through all available legal procedures—local board personal appearance, district appeal, and perhaps even a national appeal--a person may find himself still classified 1-A and facing an induction order. Many people in this circumstance have felt that they were being unjustly denied their legal right to a classification for which they were qualified, and rather than to allow the SS to break the law by denying them their legal right, have chosen to refuse induction.

It is sometimes possible to convince the local board that they have committed an error, and to persuade them to reopen your classification and reconsider it. Failing that, if you refuse induction it may be possible for your lawyer to convince the US Attorney that the local board erred, and to persuade the US Attorney not to prosecute and to send the file back to the local board with a letter recommending that your request be granted. Contact with the US Attorney won't always work, but is always worth a try.

If you end up raising the issue of your classification as a defense to a charge of refusing induction, the argument will be that the SS had no legal reason to classify you as eligible for induction in the first place.

For instance, if Brad Freeberg becomes a minister and requests a ministerial exemption (4-D) from his draft board, he has made a valid request. Say his board says that although he is an ordained minister in the Universal Life Church, he is not qualified for a 4-D classification because the Universal Life Church is not a recognized church. The board refuses to classify Brad 4-D for that reason, and so does the appeal board. Brad is issued an order to report for induction, and refuses induction.

In court Brad argues that SS regulations do not have a list of approved churches. To qualify for a 4-D exemption a man must simply be a full time minister of religion. Since Brad can prove that he serves a regular congregation of fifteen people, plus many more in his "street ministry", and that he spends an average of thirty hours a week acting as a minister, he feels qualified for a 4-D exemption. Further, he presented all of that information to the SS, but was denied an exemption by them.

Brad has a valid "basis in fact" defense.[3] The SS had no legal basis for denial of his claim, and therefore no basis in fact for his 1-A classification. Since it is illegal to order a person classified 4-D to report for induction, and since Brad has proved that he was in fact 4-D but for the board's errors, his induction order was illegal. You can't convict a man for refusing an illegal order.

The basis in fact defense has been most commonly raised in cases where claims of 1-O

200

conscientious objector status have been denied. There are literally hundreds of reported court cases in this area alone. When denying a conscientious objector claim the SS is required to give reasons for denial.[4] However, there must be a basis in fact for its reasons.[5] The courts have reviewed SS reasoning in this area and set guidelines for local boards to follow.

One common reason for denying a conscientious objector claim is the board finding that the man does not sincerely hold his stated beliefs. However, such a finding may not rest on mere disbelief by the local board.[6] A failure to use appeals or obey the law is not enough to support a finding of insincerity.[7] "Late filing" of a claim does not support a finding of insincerity as long as the claim is filed in time for local board consideration.[8] A lack of formal religious training or failure to belong to an organized church can not be a basis for denying conscientious objector status.[9] The list of invalid reasons for denial goes on and on.

In court, the person you must convince is the judge. If he or she feels that the SS wrongfully denied a classification, you will be found not guilty and the matter will be referred back to the local board, perhaps with the judge's recommendation that the board grant the classification you want. The entire case may even be thrown out of court before the trial begins. It has happened that an informal meeting in the judge's chambers or a well prepared trial brief has resulted in the case never getting to the courtroom.

Of course, if the judge feels that a man is not qualified for the classification, that he did not do everything in his power to try to get the classification granted through the system, or that the SS reason for denial is sufficient, the man may be found guilty. If, for instance, a man submitted a conscientious objector claim, was turned down by the local board, but did not appeal to the district appeal board, his chances in court are pretty bad.

The courts have consistently held since 1944 that in order for a basis in fact defense to be raised in court, a man must first have "exhausted his administrative remedies".[10] In other words, he must have used every available means to solve the problem through the system. Failure to appeal an unsatisfactory classification legally means that your have accepted that classification. For that reason, you have no right to argue in court that you should be acquitted on the basis of an ungranted classification. If you plan to go to court over an ungranted classification, you should be very sure that you are qualified for that classification and that you have done everything in your power to get the classification granted by the SS.

In the past, the basis in fact defense has worked well in cases involving ungranted claims for conscientious objector status and for hardship deferments. However, it has not had a very good track record in the area of medical exemptions. The attitude of the courts seems to be that they will not act as "super draft boards" to determine a man's eligibility for a given classification, but are willing to review whether or not a local board determination rested on some ascertainable factual basis. Thus the courts will not find a man eligible for conscientious objector status, but will find that the reasons given by the SS for denial of a conscientious objector claim are invalid if there is no factual basis for the SS findings. In the area of medical exemption the courts have consistently refused to sit as MEPS examiners, and have almost always accepted the conclusion of the MEPS regarding a man's acceptability rather than to find that MEPS erred in finding a man acceptable. Because of this, a man whose ungranted classification is a 4-F exemption may not have the same degree of success with his defense as the man whose ungranted classification is a 1-O or a 3-A.

On the other hand, the problem has often been a lack of documentation. When the defense revolves around an ungranted CO claim, the SS file will contain a written application and lots of other documentation (especially if you follow the advice in Chapters 14—16). A surprising number of people show up at MEPS seeking a 4-F exemption without a scrap of documentation. As pointed out in Chapters 12 and 13, it is usually not enough just to show up and claim that you should be given a 4-F. Doctor's letters and similar documentation are the key to getting 4-F at MEPS, and they may be crucial to your defense if MEPS finds you acceptable and you decide to refuse induction.

Constitutionality

The third kind of defense is to challenge the constitutionality of the draft. While I personally feel strongly that the Selective Service System goes directly against the United States Constitution, it must be pointed out that this line of defense has never been successful. Various issues of constitutional magnitude--such as the power of the federal government to conscript, the power to draft people to fight in undeclared wars, the infringement upon freedom of religion or freedom of speech, the infringement upon freedom of association, the prohibition of involuntary servitude, and many other points--have been raised at one time or another, and have consistently lost.[11] This line of defense will almost certainly result in a person being found guilty, unless it is used along with another line of defense.

If you are strongly convinced that the government has no right to draft you, and if you are willing to face the probability of a conviction and possible prison

sentence, you have my best wishes and firm support. Some people feel strongly that the draft is unconstitutional, and that the issue should repeatedly be raised in the courts. Others feel that constitutional issues can help make a politically charged trial and therefore act as a good means of raising social issues. I agree, but feel that the nation and court system have become increasingly conservative, so there is a very real danger of creating bad legal precedents.

Other lines of defense

Some of the defenses used in traditional criminal cases, such as lack of intent, lack of knowledge, mistake of fact, and so on, have mostly been unsuccessful in Selective Service cases. As discussed in Chapter 14, a draft registrant has a legal duty to insure that all SS mail reaches him, and that all of his mail to the SS reaches the system. Because of those duties, along with the judicial presumption of administrative regularity (a presumption that the SS has done everything correctly) and the judicial presumption that SS mail which is sent out has been received, it is extremely difficult for a draft defendant to convince a judge or jury that he did not receive a particular order without also admitting that he violated his legal duty to keep the system informed of an address where mail would reach him.

In cases involving charges other than refusing induction or failure to report for induction--such as failure to register, late registration, failure to report a change of address, and so on—it is unlikely that a defense involving procedural errors or ungranted classification would be successful. Attorneys handling such cases should study "Tigar, Selective Service Law Reporter Practice Manual," and also Veiluva, "Registration And the Military Selective Service Act." These are available from CCCO, whose addresses appear in the back of this book.

Sentencing practices

On the brighter side, not all men who violate the draft law have been prosecuted, not all men who have been prosecuted have been convicted, and not all men who have been convicted have been sentenced to prison.

During the Vietnam draft, and particularly in the later years of that draft, only a small percentage of the people who refused induction were actually prosecuted. This was no doubt in direct relation to the upsurge in the number of men filing for deferments, exemptions, and conscientious objector status. By filing such claims men made use of their procedural rights under the draft law, and in doing so allowed local boards and appeal boards to make countless procedural errors and to provide innumerable faulty reasons for denial of claims. The system was so inept at processing men for induction that literally hundreds of thousands of men who refused induction had their files returned to the local boards for further processing.

However, even though perhaps nine cases out of ten were not prosecuted, this does not mean that only one in ten **could** have been prosecuted. In many instances a man who had refused induction would find that he had virtually no defense to the charges. Rather than face an almost certain conviction and the possibility of a prison sentence, many thousands of men agreed to accept induction if re-ordered, or to enlist in order to avoid prosecution. Thus, while nine men out of ten were not prosecuted, far fewer actually succeeded in avoiding the draft and in avoiding prosecution. In reviewing the following statistics, bear in mind that not all men who had charges dropped or dismissed went free. Many of them had charges dismissed only upon a showing that they had enlisted or volunteered for induction.

During 1971 there were 2,973 men charged with violating the Selective Service Act. Of those men, 57% (1,701) had charges dismissed, 7% (217) were acquitted by a court trial, and another .6% (19) were acquitted by a jury. Roughly 35% of the men charged (1,036) were found guilty, either because they entered pleas of guilty or "no contest" (590) or because their defense failed and they were found guilty by a judge (350) or a jury (96).

Of the 1,036 men found guilty, only 377 were sentenced to prison: 79 received sentences of one year or less, 140 were given sentences of one to three years, 129 received sentences between three and five years, and 29 were sentenced to prison for five years or more. However, 63% of the men convicted (650) were given probation sentences and only nine had fines imposed. The average prison term that year was 29 months.[12]

Not surprisingly, sentencing practices have varied from court to court. In Maryland, for instance, 31 men were charged with draft law violations during fiscal year 1971, and 14 (45%) were convicted. By contrast, in the San Diego, California district court 63 men were charged with draft law violations and only 16 (25%) were found guilty. Average prison terms likewise varied from a low of 19.6 months in Oregon to a high of 41.1 months in the courts serving Maryland, the Carolinas, Virginia and West Virginia.[13]

The legal problems of draft law violators do not end with the courts or the prisons. While practices vary from state to state, most discriminate against convicted draft law violators, since they are felons. In some states, such as California, draft law violators do not lose their rights to vote, to practice law or medicine, or other rights. In other states, they lose it all.

In addition to the legal disabilities of a draft law conviction, it is also possible that a federal felony conviction on a man's record could cause employment problems. While some employers will look beyond the fact of conviction to see what charge a man was convicted of, many will treat all felons the same regardless of whether their crime was murder or refusing to murder.

In the past, draft law violators who were no longer of draft age have almost always been able to receive a Presidential pardon. Such a pardon usually will remove most or all of the restrictions on a man's rights resulting from a draft law conviction. But here again, practices vary from state to state, and from one employer to the next. Presidential pardons may be requested by filling out special forms addressed to the United States Pardon Attorney.

It is also possible for a draft violator who is not yet twenty-two years old at the time of conviction to be sentenced under the Federal Youth Corrections Act.[14] Sentencing under that Act results in an indeterminate sentence of six months to six years, although most men in the past found that their sentence under the Youth Corrections Act worked out about the same as if they had been sentenced under the Selective Service Act. A man sentenced under the Youth Corrections Act may not have the same legal disabilities imposed upon him as a man sentenced under the Selective Service Act, and will usually find that employment problems are also lessened.

For many men the possibility of conviction will persuade them to do whatever they are ordered to do. For others, following their conscience is more important than following the law. No one should refuse induction thinking he can "get away with it," that he will "get off light," or that it is an "easy way out." But then again, a violation of the law, even with its penalties, may be easier to live with in later years than a violation of your principles.

APPENDIXES

A. ALIENS AND THE DRAFT

Citizens of a country other than the United States, and all stateless persons, are considered "aliens." Aliens are required to apply to the United States government for permission to enter this country, and that permission is generally given in the form of a "visa." With few exceptions, aliens who permanently enter the United States are subject to the draft law. Even illegal aliens—people who reside in the United States without formal governmental permission—are required to register with Selective Service if they were born in 1960 or later.

In some cases aliens and "dual nationals" (people who are citizens of the United States and another country) are treated differently by the draft law than are United States citizens. Because of the complex regulations issued by the Department of State and the Immigration and Naturalization Service (INS), aliens and dual nationals may find their options under the draft law limited. On the other hand, there are two special draft classifications that are available only to aliens and dual nationals: Class 4-C and Class 4-T.

Because of the complex interplay between Selective Service regulations and INS regulations, if you are an alien or a dual national, your draft counselor should work closely with an immigration attorney to insure that you don't endanger your visa or residency status.

If you are an alien legally in the United States, you were admitted under one of several different kinds of visa. If you intend to settle in this country, you were probably admitted on a permanent resident visa, sometimes called "immigrant status." Or you may have been admitted on a temporary visa that restricts your stay in the United States to a particular purpose, such as visiting, going to school, diplomatic work, and so on.

In some cases Canadian and British subjects with homes in those countries, Mexican nationals, and many nationals from the Carribean area are admitted into the United States as non-immigrants without visas. If you are in this group, your draft status is the same as if you were admitted on the type of visa appropriate to the purpose of your visit. In addition, some refugees and other people are admitted on "parole" or "conditional entry" status. In practice, the SS treats such people as permanent residents.

Dual citizenship is only recognized in the United States if you were entitled to both citizenships at birth. A United States citizen is almost always considered to have renounced his United States citizenship by accepting citizenship in another country, and is thereafter treated as an alien by the United States government. Both dual nationals and ex-US citizens are likely to be subject to the draft, either because of their United States citizenship or because they are aliens permanently residing in the United States.

Aliens who need not register for the draft

Non-immigrant aliens admitted to the United States on a temporary visa are not required to register for the draft.[1] The following are some of the groups most commonly falling into this category:

1. **Tourists** and visitors for pleasure.

2. **Students** in full-time programs approved by the Attorney General and the Office of Education, and their spouses and minor

212

children, as long as they continue as satisfactory students.

3. **Exchange program participants** under the Mutual Educational and Cultural Exchange Act, and their spouses and minor children, as long as they continue in such programs.

4. **Alien doctors** here as exchange visitors.

5. **Temporary or seasonal workers** who have entered the United States under an agreement with a foreign government or agency, as long as they continue on the job.

6. **Foreign executives and technical personnel** of international corporations who enter the United States temporarily to work for the same employers.

7. **Visitors for business,** including "treaty traders" --foreign businessmen and investors admitted under commercial treaties.

8. **Foreign press representatives** in the United States temporarily for media activities.

9. **Officials** such as ambassadors, consuls, and other employees of foreign governments and of international public organizations, such as the United Nations. Representatives of foreign governments admitted without visas are also exempt from draft registration.

10. **Aliens in transit** through the United States, crewmen, fiancees of United States citizens allowed here 90 days in advance of marriage.

11. **Treaty aliens** are aliens from a country having a treaty with the United States exempting aliens from military service, **so long as** not admitted on permanent resident status.

There are fifteen treaty countries involved: Argentina, Austria, Costa Rica, Estonia, Formosa, Honduras, Ireland, Italy, Latvia, Liberia, Norway, Paraguay, Spain, Switzerland, Yugoslavia.

If you are in one of the categories above, you should keep an official document in your possession showing that you are exempt from draft registration. For most men admitted on the types of visas listed above, the visa itself or its equivalent should suffice. For foreign diplomats, the Department of State form will work. For certain temporary workers, an INS form will have been issued. Besides carrying documentation to protect against harassment for non-registration, a person exempt from draft registration has no other draft liability unless he changes his status to a type requiring draft registration. Normally this happens only when someone admitted on a temporary visa gains permanent resident status or becomes an illegal alien.

Aliens with selective service obligations

Any male alien admitted to the United States who is not in one of the exempt groups listed above, and all illegal aliens, must register for the draft if in an age group where registration is required.[2] Immigrant aliens admitted to the United States for permanent residence must register.

If you are an alien of draft age who entered the United States as a non-immigrant and then applied for permanent resident status, the INS may require you to register with the SS before the change of status is finally approved. Whether that happens or not, you are legally required to register.

Most permanent resident aliens are subject to almost the same rules regarding deferments, exemptions,

214

and induction into the United States military as United States citizens. Like other registrants, aliens who must register are legally required to report address changes and other material changes in their status.[3]

The draft law says that an alien can not be inducted unless he has resided in the United States for at least one year.[4] The catch is that every day you **ever** lived here counts cumulatively. If you lived in the US for six months when you were fifteen, another two months when you were seventeen, and have now lived here five months, you meet the one year requirement. It does not matter how old you were when you lived here, and it also doesn't matter whether you were here on a temporary or permanent visa. However, if you are sent an induction order before your first year in the US runs out, you are entitled to a 4-C classification. For more on 4-C, see below.

Deferments and exemptions for aliens

If you are an alien or dual national required to register with the SS, you may apply for any of the deferments or exemptions discussed throughout this book. In addition, you may qualify for one of the special classifications that apply only to aliens or dual nationals. This section discusses those special classes as well as some points an alien should consider before applying for some of the other classifications.

Conscientious Objection: There are no legal reasons why an alien can not apply for either CO classification. Aliens who are seeking US citizenship may choose from three different versions of the required "loyalty oath." The usual oath contains a promise to bear arms on behalf of the US, but alien conscientious objectors may swear instead to "perform noncombatant service in the Armed Forces of the United States when required by law," or to "perform work of national importance under civilian direction when required by law."[5] These two alternative oaths correspond to Class 1-A-O and Class 1-O standards.

The real problem for alien COs may be that a CO applicant needs to communicate his beliefs, orally and in writing, clearly enough to convince a local board that he qualifies. If English is your second language, you may want to get help from an interpreter. You have the right to have an interpreter present at the local board hearing.[6]

Dependency: The 3-A classification presents a two-edged sword for aliens. Perhaps you can make a strong claim for deferment if you often act as the family interpreter, assist with chores which require the ability to speak fluent English, if you are the one that fills out the mountain of forms that are required by life in the US, or if you fill the traditional eldest son role found in many Eastern and European cultures. However, an application for 3-A status based on **financial** dependency could cause problems for your family, especially if they are non-citizens. Under INS law, aliens can be excluded from the US if they are "likely at any time to become public charges."[7]

Class 4-F: Some of the reasons that could get you a 4-F exemption could also result in your being excluded or deported from the US. For example, under INS law you can be excluded from the US if you are a narcotics addict or an alcoholic, if you have a contagious disease, if you have a physical defect that may affect your ability to earn a living, or if you are mentally retarded.[8] Similarly, gay non-citizens may run into the long-standing INS policy that gays are excludable as "sexual deviates."[9] There have been recent legal challenges to that policy, including at least one ruling that aliens can not lawfully be excluded merely for being gay.[10] However, the INS still maintains a contrary opinion, and it remains to be seen whether they will finally emerge from the dark ages.

Veterans: In addition to the usual exemption for having served in the US military, aliens, dual nationals, and naturalized US citizens may qualify for a 4-A exemption for having served at least twelve months' active duty in the armed forces of a country listed in the next paragraph. "Active duty" is as defined by the foreign country. In some countries, such as Mexico, you may be able to get a certificate verifying military service even though your "active duty" was only on paper, and you were really merely available for weekend drills. The key to this exemption is to obtain a certificate of service, written in English, from your country's diplomatic mission or local consular offices.

The veteran's exemption nations are: Argentina, Australia, Barbados, Belgium, Bolivia, Brazil, Canada, Chile, Formosa, Columbia, Costa Rica, Denmark, Dominican Republic, Ecuador, El Salvador, France, Federal Republic of Germany, Greece, Guatemala, Haiti, Honduras, Iceland, Iran, Italy, Jamaica, Japan, South Korea, Luxembourg, Mexico, Netherlands, New Zealand, Nicaragua, Norway, Pakistan, Panama, Paraguay, Peru, Philippines, Portugal, Spain, Thailand, Trinidad & Tobago, Turkey, United Kingdom, Uruguay, Venezuela, South Vietnam.

Class 4-C: This classification applies only to non-citizens and dual nationals. It actually covers several different situations.

As mentioned above, you can not be inducted if you have been in the United States less than one year. In such a case you are automatically entitled to be classified 4-C. Since class 4-C is a deferment, you will continue to move through the Age Selection Groups if your 4-C lasts beyond the end of the calendar year. Thus if you are inducted in September when you have only been in the US for six months, you are entitled to a 4-C deferment. By the time it expires, you will be in the next Age Selection Group and can not be re-ordered for induction unless other members of that group are also being called up.

Class 4-C also applies to non-citizens who have registered with the SS but are currently outside the country, provided that they are not already under an induction or alternate service order.[11] For example, if you registered with the SS but are currently going to school or working outside the US, you qualify for Class 4-C. However, there may be a risk of losing your permanent resident status if you remain outside the US for more than one year. The INS may conclude that your prolonged absence is an abandonment of your residence in the US, and you could be excluded and required to re-apply before being admitted back into the country.

Another risk is that you can be excluded if the INS concludes that you have "departed from or remained outside the United States to avoid or evade" the draft.[12] One way to protect yourself from that problem might be to carefully document that your reason for leaving the country was other than draft avoidance, such as if you were outside the US to go to school or to take a particular job.

Yet another aspect of the 4-C classification applies if your job status would entitle you to a specific non-immigrant visa. You are entitled to a 4-C classification so long as you hold that job, without having to give up your residency.[15] Generally this will apply to investors, diplomats, and employees of certain international organizations such as the United Nations.

The 4-C classification is also available to dual nationals whose other country has a treaty with the US that provides for exemption from military service. These countries are: Australia, Austria, Belgium, Brazil, Columbia, Cuba, Cyprus, El Salvador, Finland, India, Indonesia, Malawi, Malta, Maurutania, Mauritius, Netherlands, Niger, Nigeria, South Africa, Swazililand, Sweden, United Kingdom.

One odd-ball provision of the 4-C classification applies to people who register with the SS and then acquire a status which exempts them from registration.[13] This confusing provision applies only to non-citizens who are non-immigrants as well. In other words, you would have to give up permanent resident status in order to qualify; it is unlikely that the INS would allow such a status change, and even if allowed it could make you ineligible for US citizenship.[14]

Class 4-T: This classification was formerly covered under Class 4-C, but was made separate in 1982. This is an exemption for aliens whose country has a treaty with the United States which exempts citizens from military service in the US.[16] Some dual nationals may qualify for both the 4-T and 4-C classifications. If so, the 4-C is probably a better deal, since being classified 4-T makes you ineligible for US citizenship.[17] In the past, aliens who requested this exemption have been barred from citizenship even though they later entered the military voluntarily.[18] You cannot be forced to accept a 4-T classification because to qualify for it you must specifically give up your right to US citizenship.[19] The countries whose citizens qualify for a 4-T exemption are: Argentina, Austria, Costa Rica, Estonia, Formosa, Honduras, Ireland, Italy, Latvia, Liberia, Norway, Paraguay, Spain, Switzerland, Yugoslavia.

Special problems for aliens

Aliens who are illegally inside the United States face special problems. If the SS discovers illegal aliens, they are reported to INS. As crazy as it may seem, the SS has taken the position that undocumented workers and other illegal aliens are required to register and are eligible for induction. The SS has been known to issue an induction order to an undocumented alien while waiting to see whether the INS will bring a deportation proceeding. Failure to register or refusal of induction could result in a prosecution for violation of the draft law, or deportation, or both.

Even non-citizens who have visas or permanent residence status may face dire consequences for draft resistance. In addition to the penalties faced by citizens, non-citizens must also deal with the INS. Because of the extensive governmental intrusion into the lives of non-citizens, it is almost impossible to believe that an alien non-registrant would go undetected. It is also possible that the INS could bring deportation proceedings against an alien who refused to register, refused induction, or otherwise violated the draft law.

It is up to the consular service of the State Department to issue visas and to interpret the "inadmissible classes" section of the immigration law. At the border and within the United States, an alien must deal with the Immigration and Naturalization Service. For example, under a recent change to INS law, an alien can be kept from leaving the US if he is of registration age, unless he can show proof that he has registered with the SS.[20] An immigration lawyer is often helpful, and is really necessary in cases involving deportation, private bills, and many other immigration matters.

B. COUNSELING AGENCIES

These agencies are in touch with draft counseling activities throughout the nation. You can write to them for information about draft laws, forms, or for referral to a draft counselor or lawyer in your vicinity.

CENTRAL COMMITTEE FOR
CONSCIENTIOUS OBJECTORS (CCCO)
    2208 South Street
    Philadelphia, PA 19146
    215/ 545-4626
       or
    1251 Second Avenue
    San Francisco, CA 94122
    415/ 566-0500

NATIONAL INTER-RELIGIOUS SERVICE BOARD
FOR CONSCIENTIOUS OBJECTORS (NISBCO)
    550 Washington Building
    15th and New York Avenue NW
    Washington, DC 20005

MIDWEST COMMITTEE FOR
MILITARY AND DRAFT COUNSELING
    59 East Van Buren, Room 508
    Chicago, IL 60605
    312/ 939-3349

C. MEDICAL STANDARDS

CHAPTER 2
MEDICAL FITNESS STANDARDS FOR APPOINTMENT, ENLISTMENT, AND INDUCTION
(Short Title: PROCUREMENT MEDICAL FITNESS STANDARDS)

Section I. GENERAL

2-1. Scope

This chapter sets forth the medical conditions and physical defects which are causes for rejection for military service in peacetime. For medical fitness standards during mobilization, see chapter 6.

2-2. Applicability

a. These standards apply to—

(1) *Applicants for appointment as commissioned or warrant officers* in the Active Army, Army National Guard, and Army Reserve. (Special categories of personnel, such as physicians, dentists, and other specialists, will be procured under standards prescribed by the Secretary of the Army in appropriate personnel procurement program directives.)

★(2) *Applicants for enlistment.*

(3) *Civilian applicants for enlistment in the Regular Army.* These standards are applicable until enlistees have completed 4 months of active duty for medical conditions or physical defects that existed prior to original enlistment. (See also AR 635–40 and AR 635–200.)

(4) *Members of units of the Army National Guard or Army Reserve who apply for enlistment in the Regular Army* or who reenter active duty for training under the "split training" option must meet the standards of medical fitness prescribed by chapter 3. (See also para 3–2a(2) of this regulation, and AR 601–210 for administrative procedures for separation for medically unfitting conditions that existed prior to enlistment.)

(5) *Civilian applicants for enlistment in the Army National Guard and Army Reserve.* These standards are applicable until the enlistees have completed an initial period of active duty for training and return to their Reserve Component unit for medical conditions or physical defects that existed prior to original en-

listment. (See also AR 635–40, AR 635–200, and AR 135–178.)

(6) *Applicants for reenlistment* in the Active Army, Army National Guard, and Army Reserve after a period of more than 6 months has elapsed since discharge.

(7) *Applicants for the Advanced Course Army ROTC,* and other personnel procurement programs, other than induction, for which these standards are prescribed.

(8) *Retention of cadets* of the United States Military Academy, students enrolled in the Uniformed Services University of Health Sciences, and the Army ROTC programs, except for such conditions that have been diagnosed since entrance into the Academy, University or the ROTC programs. With respect to such conditions, upon recommendation of the Surgeon, United States Military Academy (for USMA cadets), the President, Uniformed Services University of Health Sciences (for students enrolled in that institution), or the Surgeon, United States Army Training and Doctrine Command (for ROTC cadets), the medical fitness standards of chapter 3 are applicable for retention in the Academy, the University of Health Sciences, the ROTC programs, appointment or enlistment, and entrance on active duty or active duty for training in a commissioned or enlisted status.

(9) *Registrants who undergo preinduction or induction medical examination,* except physicians, dentists and allied medical specialists who are to be evaluated under chapter 8.

(10) *Male applicants for enlistment in the US Air Force.*

(11) *Male applicants for nonprior service enlistment in the US Navy or Naval Reserve.*

(12) *"Changeable accessions" for enlistment* in the US Marine Corps or Marine Corps Reserve.

b. This publication does not contain information that affects the New Manning System.

2–3. Abdominal Organs and Gastrointestinal System

The causes for rejection for appointment, enlistment, and induction are—

a. *Cholecystectomy*, sequelae of, such as postoperative stricture of the common bile duct, reforming of stones in hepatic or common bile ducts, or incisional hernia, or postcholecystectomy syndrome when symptoms are so severe as to interfere with normal performance of duty.

b. *Cholecystitis*, acute or chronic, with or without cholelithiasis, if diagnosis is confirmed by usual laboratory procedures or authentic medical records.

c. *Cirrhosis* regardless of the absence of manifestations such as jaundice, ascites, or known esophageal varices, abnormal liver function tests with or without history of chronic alcoholism.

d. *Fistula* in ano.

e. *Gastritis*, chronic hypertrophic, severe.

f. *Hemorrhoids*.

(1) External hemorrhoids producing marked symptoms.

(2) Internal hemorrhoids, if large or accompanied with hemorrhage or protruding intermittently or constantly.

g. *Hepatitis* within the preceding 6 months, or persistence of symptoms after a reasonable period of time with objective evidence of impairment of liver function.

h. *Hernia*.

(1) Hernia other than small asymptomatic umbilical or hiatal.

(2) History of operation for hernia within the preceding 60 days.

i. *Intestinal obstruction* or authenticated history of more than one episode, if either occurred during the preceding 5 years or if resulting condition remains which produces significant symptoms or requires treatment.

j. *Megacolon* of more than minimal degree, *diverticulitis, regional enteritis, and ulcerative colitis. Irritable colon* of more than moderate degree.

k. *Pancreas*, acute or chronic disease of, if proven by laboratory tests, or authenticated medical records.

l. *Rectum*, stricture of prolapse of.

m. *Resection, gastric or of bowel; or gastroenterostomy;* however, minimal intestinal resection in infancy or childhood (for example: for intussusception or pyloric stenosis) is acceptable if the individual has been asymptomatic since the resection and if surgical consultation (to include upper and lower gastrointestinal series) gives complete clearance.

n. *Scars*.

(1) Scars, abdominal, regardless of cause, which show hernial bulging or which interfere with movements.

(2) Scar pain associated with disturbance of function of abdominal wall or contained viscera.

o. *Sinuses* of the abdominal wall.

p. *Splenectomy*, except when accomplished for the following:

(1) Trauma.

(2) Causes unrelated to diseases of the spleen.

(3) Hereditary spherocytosis.

(4) Disease involving the spleen when followed by correction of the condition for a period of at least 2 years.

q. *Tumors*. See paragraphs 2–40 and 2–41.

r. *Ulcer*.

(1) Ulcer of the stomach or duodenum if diagnosis is confirmed by X-ray examination, or authenticated history thereof.

(2) Authentic history of surgical operation(s) for gastric or duodenal ulcer.

★s. *Other* congenital or acquired abnormalities such as gastrointestinal bypass or stomach stapling for control of obesity; and defects which preclude satisfactory performance of military duty or which require frequent and prolonged treatment.

Section III. BLOOD AND BLOOD-FORMING TISSUE DISEASES

2–4. Blood and Blood-Forming Tissue Diseases

The causes for rejection for appointment, enlistment and induction are—

a. *Anemia:*
(1) Blood loss anemia—until both condition and basic cause are corrected.
(2) Deficiency anemia, not controlled by medication.
(3) Abnormal destruction of RBC's: hemolytic anemia.
(4) Faulty RBC construction: Hereditary hemolytic anemia, thalassemia, and sickle cell disease.
(5) Myelophthisic anemia: myelomatosis, leukemia, Hodgkin's disease.
(6) Primary refractory anemia: aplastic anemia, DiGuglielmo's syndrome.
b. *Hemorrhagic states:*

(1) Due to changes in coagulation system (hemophilia, etc.).
(2) Due to platelet deficiency.
(3) Due to vascular instability.
c. *Leukopenia,* chronic or recurrent, associated with increased susceptibility to infection.
d. *Myeloproliferative disease (other than leukemia):*
(1) Myelofibrosis.
(2) Megakaryocytic myelosis.
(3) Polycythemia vera.
e. *Splenomegaly* until the cause is remedied.
f. *Thromboembolic disease* except for acute, nonrecurrent conditions.

Section IV. DENTAL

2-5. Dental

The causes for rejection for appointment, enlistment, and induction are—
a. *Diseases of the jaws or associated tissues* which are not easily remediable and which will incapacitate the individual or prevent the satisfactory performance of military duty.
b. *Malocclusion,* severe, which interferes with the mastication of a normal diet.

c. *Oral tissues,* extensive loss of, in an amount that would prevent replacement of missing teeth with a satisfactory prosthetic appliance.
d. *Orthodontic appliances.* See special administrative criteria in paragraph 7-16.
e. *Relationship between the mandible and maxilla* of such a nature as to preclude future satisfactory prosthodontic replacement.

Section V. EARS AND HEARING

2-6. Ears

The causes for rejection for appointment, enlistment, and induction are—
a. *Auditory canal.*
(1) Atresia or severe stenosis of the external auditory canal.
(2) Tumors of the external auditory canal except mild exostoses.
(3) Severe external otitis, acute or chronic.
b. *Auricle.* Agenesis, severe; or severe traumatic deformity, unilateral or bilateral.
c. *Mastoids.*
(1) Mastoiditis, acute or chronic.
(2) Residual or mastoid operation with marked external deformity which precludes or interferes with the wearing of a gas mask or helmet.
(3) Mastoid fistula.
d. *Meniere's syndrome.*
e. *Middle ear.*

(1) Acute or chronic suppurative otitis media. Individuals with a recent history of acute suppurative otitis media will not be accepted unless the condition is healed and a sufficient interval of time subsequent to treatment has elapsed to insure that the disease is in fact not chronic.
(2) Adhesive otitis media associated with hearing level by audiometric test of 20 dB or more average for the speech frequencies (500, 1000, and 2000 cycles per second) in either ear regardless of the hearing level in the other ear.
(3) Acute or chronic serous otitis media.
(4) Presence of ,attic perforation in which presence of cholesteatoma is suspected.
(5) Repeated attacks of catarrhal otitis media; intact greyish, thickened drum(s).
f. *Tympanic membrane.*
(1) Any perforation of the tympanic membrane.
(2) Severe scarring of the tympanic membrane associated with hearing level by

225

audiometric test of 20 dB or more average for the speech frequencies (500, 1000, and 2000 cycles per second) in either ear regardless of the hearing level in the other ear.

g. Other diseases and defects of the ear which obviously preclude satisfactory performance of duty or which require frequent and prolonged treatment.

2–7. Hearing

(See also para 2–6.)

The cause for rejection for appointment, enlistment, and induction is—

Hearing threshold level greater than that described in table I, appendix II.

Section VI. ENDOCRINE AND METABOLIC DISORDERS

2–8. Endocrine and Metabolic Disorders

The causes for rejection for appointment, enlistment, and induction are—
 a. Adrenal gland, malfunction of, of any degree.
 b. Cretinism.
 c. Diabetes insipidus.
 d. Diabetes mellitus.
 e. Gigantism or acromegaly.
 f. Glycosuria, persistent, regardless of cause.
 g. Goiter.
 (1) Simple goiter with definite pressure symptoms or so large in size as to interfere with the wearing of a military uniform or military equipment.
 (2) *Thyrotoxicosis.*

h. Gout.
 i. Hyperinsulinism, confirmed, symptomatic.
 j. Hyperparathyroidism and hypoparathyroidism.
 k. Hypopituitarism, severe.
 l. Myxedema, spontaneous or postoperative (with clinical manifestations and not based solely on low basal metabolic rate).
 m. Nutritional deficiency diseases (including sprue, beriberi, pellagra, and scurvy) which are more than mild and not readily remediable or in which permanent pathological changes have been established.
 n. Other endocrine or metabolic disorders which obviously preclude satisfactory performance of duty or which require frequent and prolonged treatment.

Section VII. EXTREMITIES

2–9. Upper Extremities
 (See para 2–11.)

The causes for rejection for appointment, enlistment, and induction are—
 a. Limitation of motion. An individual will be considered unacceptable if the joint ranges of motion are less than the measurements listed below (TM 8–640).
 (1) *Shoulder.*
 (a) Forward elevation to 90°.
 (b) Abduction to 90°.
 (2) *Elbow.*
 (a) Flexion to 100°.
 (b) Extension to 15°.
 (3) *Wrist.* A total range of 15° (extension plus flexion).
 (4) *Hand.*
 (a) Pronation to the first quarter of normal arc.

 (b) Supination to the first quarter of the normal arc.
 (5) *Fingers.* Inability to clench fist, pick up a pin or needle, and grasp an object.
 b. Hand and fingers.
 (1) Absence (or loss) of more than 1/3 of the distal phalanx of either thumb.
 (2) Absence (or loss) of distal and middle phalanx of an index, middle or ring finger of either hand irrespective of the absence (or loss) of little finger.
 (2.1) Absence of more than the distal phalanx of any two of the following fingers, index, middle finger or ring finger, of either hand.
 (3) Absence of hand or any portion thereof except for fingers as noted above.
 (4) *Hyperdactylia.*
 (5) Scars and deformities of the fingers and/or hand which impair circulation, are symp-

tomatic, are so disfiguring as to make the individual objectionable in ordinary social relationships, or which impair normal function to such a degree as to interfere with the satisfactory performance of military duty.

c. *Wrist, forearm, elbow, arm, and shoulder.* Healed disease or injury of wrist, elbow, or shoulder with residual weakness or symptoms of such a degree as to preclude satisfactory performance of duty.

2-10. Lower Extremities
(See para 2-11.)

The causes for rejection for appointment, enlistment, and induction are—

a. *Limitation of motion.* An individual will be considered unacceptable if the joint ranges of motion are less than the measurements listed below (TM 8-640).

(1) *Hip.*
　(a) Flexion to 90°.
　(b) Extension to 10° (beyond 0).
(2) *Knee.*
　(a) Full extension.
　(b) Flexion to 90°.
(3) *Ankle.*
　(a) Dorsiflexion to 10°.
　(b) Plantar flexion to 10°.
(4) *Toes.* Stiffness which interferes with walking, marching, running, or jumping.

b. *Foot and ankle.*

(1) Absence of one or more small toes of one or both feet, if function of the foot is poor or running or jumping is precluded, or absence of a foot or any portion thereof except for toes as noted herein.

(2) Absence (or loss) of great toe(s) or loss of dorsal flexion thereof if function of the foot is impaired.

(3) Claw toes precluding the wearing of combat service boots.

(4) Clubfoot.

(5) Flatfoot, pronounced cases, with decided eversion of the foot and marked bulging of the inner border, due to inward rotation of the astragalus, regardless of the presence or absence of symptoms.

(6) Flatfoot, spastic.

(7) Hallux valgus, if severe and associated with marked extostosis or bunion.

(8) Hammer toe which interferes with the wearing of combat service boots.

(9) Healed disease, injury, or deformity including hyperdactylia which precludes running, is accompanied by disabling pain, or which prohibits wearing of combat service boots.

(10) Ingrowing toe nails, if severe, and not remediable.

(11) Obliteration of the transverse arch associated with permanent flexion of the small toes.

(12) Pes cavus, with contracted plantar fascia, dorsiflexed toes, tenderness under the metatarsal heads, and callosity under the weight-bearing areas.

c. *Leg, knee, thigh, and hip.*

(1) Dislocated semilunar cartilage, loose or foreign bodies within the knee joint, or history of surgical correction of same if—

　(a) Within the preceding 6 months.

　(b) Six months or more have elapsed since operation without recurrence, and there is instability of the knee ligaments in lateral or anteroposterior directions in comparison with the normal knee or abnormalities noted on X-ray, there is significant atrophy or weakness of the thigh musculature in comparison with the normal side, there is not acceptable active motion in flexion and extension, or there are other symptoms of internal derangement.

(2) Authentic history or physical findings of an unstable or internally deranged joint causing disabling pain or seriously limiting function. Individuals with verified episodes of buckling or locking of the knee who have not undergone satisfactory surgical correction or if, subsequent to surgery, there is evidence of more than mild instability of the knee ligaments in lateral and anteroposterior directions in comparison with the normal knee, weakness or atrophy of the thigh musculature in comparison with the normal side, or if the individual requires medical treatment of sufficient frequency to interfere with the performance of military duty.

d. *General.*

(1) Deformities of one or both lower extremities which have interfered with function to such a degree as to prevent the individual from following a *physically active* vocation in civilian life or which would interfere with the satisfacto-

ry completion of prescribed training and performance of military duty.

(2) Diseases or deformities of the hip, knee,or ankle joint which interfere with walking, running, or weight bearing.

(3) Pain in the lower back or leg which is intractable and disabling to the degree of interfering with walking, running, and weight bearing.

(4) Shortening of a lower extremity resulting in any limp of noticeable degree.

2-11. Miscellaneous
(See also paras 2-9 and 2-10.)

The causes for rejection for appointment, enlistment, and induction are—

a. Arthritis.

★(1) Active or subacute arthritis.

(2) Chronic osteoarthritis or traumatic arthritis of isolated joints of more than minimal degree, which has interfered with the following of a physically active vocation in civilian life or which precludes the satisfactory performance of military duty.

★(3) Documented clinical history of rheumatoid arthritis, including Strumpell-Marie type.

(4) Traumatic arthritis of a major joint of more than minimal degree.

b. Disease of any bone or joint, healed, with such resulting deformity or rigidity that function is impaired to such a degree that it will interfere with military service.

c. Dislocation, old unreduced; substantiated history of recurrent dislocations of major joints; instability of a major joint, symptomatic and more than mild; or if, subsequent to surgery, there is evidence of more than mild instability in comparison with the normal joint, weakness or atrophy in comparison with the normal side, or if the individual requires medical treatment of sufficient frequency to interfere with the performance of military duty.

d. Fractures.

(1) Malunited fractures that interfere significantly with function.

(2) Ununited fractures.

(3) Any old or recent fracture in which a plate, pin, or screws were used for fixation and left in place and which may be subject to easy trauma; i.e., as a plate tibia, etc.

e. Injury of a bone or joint within the preceding 6 weeks, without fracture or dislocation, of more than a minor nature.

f. Muscular paralysis, contracture, or atrophy, if progressive or of sufficient degree to interfere with military service.

f.1. Myotonia congenita. Confirmed.

g. Osteomyelitis, active or recurrent, of any bone or substantiated history of osteomyelitis of any of the long bones unless successfully treated 2 or more years previously without subsequent recurrence or disqualifying sequelae as demonstrated by both clinical and X-ray evidence.

h. Osteoporosis.

i. Scars, extensive, deep, or adherent, of the skin and soft tissues or neuromas of an extremity which are painful, which interfere with muscular movements, which preclude the wearing of military equipment, or that show a tendency to break down.

j. Chondromalacia, manifested by verified history of joint effusion, interference with function, or residuals from surgery.

Section VIII. EYES AND VISION

2-12. Eyes

The causes for rejection for appointment, enlistment, and induction are—

a. Lids.

(1) Blepharitis, chronic more than mild. Cases of acute blepharitis will be rejected until cured.

(2) Blepharospasm.

(3) Dacryocystitis, acute or chronic.

'4) Destruction of the lids, complete or extensive, sufficient to impair protection of the eye from exposure.

(5) Disfiguring cicatrices and adhesions of the eyelids to each other or to the eyeball.

(6) Growth or tumor of the eyelid other than small early basal cell tumors of the eyelid, which can be cured by treatment, and small nonprogressive asymptomatic benign lesions. See also paragraphs 2-40 and 2-41.

(7) Marked inversion or eversion of the eye-

2-6

228

lids sufficient to cause unsightly appearance or watering of eyes (entropion or ectropion).

(8) Lagophthalmos.

(9) Ptosis interfering with vision.

(10) Trichiasis, severe.

b. Conjunctiva.

(1) Conjunctivitis, chronic, including vernal catarrh and trachoma. Individuals with acute conjunctivitis are unacceptable until the condition is cured.

(2) Pterygium:

(a) Pterygium recurring after three operative procedures.

(b) Pterygium encroaching on the cornea in excess of 3 millimeters or interfering with vision.

c. Cornea.

(1) Dystrophy, corneal, of any type including keratoconus of any degree.

(2) Keratitis, acute or chronic.

(3) Ulcer, corneal; history of recurrent ulcers or corneal abrasions (including herpetic ulcers).

(4) Vascularization or opacification of the cornea from any cause which is progressive or reduces vision below the standards prescribed in paragraph 2–13.

d. Uveal tract. Inflammation of the uveal tract except healed traumatic choroiditis.

e. Retina.

(1) Angiomatoses, phakomatoses, retinal cysts, and other congenito-hereditary conditions that impair visual function.

(2) Degenerations of the retina to include macular cysts, holes, and other degenerations (hereditary or acquired degenerative changes) and other conditions affecting the macula. All types of pigmentary degenerations (primary and secondary).

(3) Detachment of the retina or history of surgery for same.

(4) Inflammation of the retina (retinitis or other inflammatory conditions of the retina to include Coats' disease, diabetic retinopathy, Eales' disease, and retinitis proliferans).

f. Optic nerve.

(1) Congenito-hereditary conditions of the optic nerve or any other central nervous system pathology affecting the efficient function of the optic nerve.

(2) Optic neuritis, neuroretinitis, or secondary optic atrophy resulting therefrom or documented history of attacks of retrobulbar neuritis.

(3) Optic atrophy (primary or secondary).

(4) Papilledema.

g. Lens.

(1) Aphakia (unilateral or bilateral).

(2) Dislocation, partial or complete, of a lens.

(3) Opacities of the lens which interfere with vision or which are considered to be progressive.

h. Ocular mobility and motility.

(1) Diplopia, documented, constant or intermittent from any cause or of any degree interfering with visual function (i.e., may suppress).

(2) Diplopia, monocular, documented, interfering with visual function.

(3) Nystagmus, with both eyes fixing, congenital or acquired.

(4) Strabismus of 40 prism diopters or more, uncorrectable by lenses to less than 40 diopters.

(5) Strabismus of any degree accompanied by documented diplopia.

(6) Strabismus, surgery for the correction of, within the preceding 6 months.

i. Miscellaneous defects and diseases.

(1) Abnormal conditions of the eye or visual fields due to diseases of the central nervous system.

(2) Absence of an eye.

(3) Asthenopia severe.

(4) Exophthalmos, unilateral or bilateral.

(5) Glaucoma, primary or secondary.

(6) Hemianopsia of any type.

(7) Loss of normal pupillary reflex reactions to light or accommodation to distance or Adie's syndrome.

(8) Loss of visual fields due to organic disease.

(9) Night blindness associated with objective disease of the eye. Verified congenital night blindness.

(10) Residuals of old contusions, lacerations, penetrations, etc., which impair visual function required for satisfactory performance of military duty.

2–7

229

(11) Retained intra-ocular foreign body.

(12) Tumors. See a(6) above and paragraphs 2–40 and 2–41.

(13) Any organic disease of the eye or adnexa not specified above which threatens continuity of vision or impairment of visual function.

2–13. Vision

★The causes of medical rejection for appointment, enlistment, and induction are listed below. The special administrative criteria for officer assignment to Armor, Artillery, Infantry, Corps of Engineers, Military Intelligence, Signal Corps, and Military Police Corps are listed in paragraph 7–19.

a. *Distant visual acuity.* Distant visual acuity of any degree which does not correct with spectacle lenses to at least one of the following:

(1) 20/40 in one eye and 20/70 in the other eye.

(2) 20/30 in one eye and 20/100 in the other eye.

(3) 20/20 in one eye and 20/400 in the other eye.

★b. *Near visual acuity.* Near visual acuity of any degree which does not correct to at least J–6 or 20/40 in the better eye.

★c. *Refractive error.* Any degree of refractive error in spherical equivalent of over −8.00 or +8.00; or if ordinary spectacles cause discomfort by reason of ghost images, prismatic displacement, etc.; if an ophthalmological consultation reveals a condition which is disqualifying; or if refractive error is corrected by orthokeratology or radial keratotomy.

d. *Contact lens.* Complicated cases requiring contact lens for adequate correction of vision as keratoconus, corneal scars, and irregular astigmatism.

Section IX. GENITOURINARY SYSTEM

2–14. Genitalia
(See also paras 2–40 and 2–41.)

The causes for rejection for appointment, enlistment, and induction are—

a. *Bartholinitis,* Bartholin's cyst.

b. *Cervicitis,* acute or chronic manifested by leukorrhea.

c. *Dysmenorrhea,* incapacitating to a degree which necessitates recurrent absences of more than a few hours from routine activities.

d. *Endometriosis,* or confirmed history thereof.

e. *Hermaphroditism.*

f. *Menopausal syndrome,* either physiologic or artificial if manifested by more than mild constitutional or mental symptoms, or artificial menopause if less than 13 months have elapsed since cessation of menses. In all cases of artificial menopause, the clinical diagnosis will be reported; if accomplished by surgery, the pathologic report will be obtained and recorded.

g. *Menstrual cycle,* irregularities of, including menorrhagia, if excessive; metrorrhagia; polymenorrhea; amenorrhea, except as noted in f above.

h. *New growths of the internal or external genitalia* except single uterine fibroid, subse-

rous, asymptomatic, less than 3 centimeters in diameter, with no general enlargement of the uterus. See also paragraphs 2–40 and 2–41.

i. *Oophoritis,* acute or chronic.

j. *Ovarian cysts,* persistent and considered to be of clinical significance.

k. *Pregnancy.*

l. *Salpingitis,* acute or chronic.

m. *Testicle(s).* (See also paras 2–40 and 2–41.)

(1) Absence or nondescent of both testicles.

(2) Undiagnsed enlargement or mass of testicle or epididymis.

(3) Undescended testicle.

n. *Urethritis,* acute or chronic, other than gonorrheal urethritis without complications.

o. *Uterus.*

(1) Cervical polyps, cervical ulcer, or marked erosion.

(2) Endocervicitis, more than mild.

(3) Generalized enlargement of the uterus due to any cause.

(4) Malposition of the uterus if more than mildly symptomatic.

p. *Vagina.*

(1) Congenital abnormalities or severe lacerations of the vagina.

(2) Vaginitis, acute or chronic, manifested by leukorrhea.

2–8

q. *Varicocele or hydrocele*, if large or painful.

r. *Vulva*.

(1) Leukoplakia.

(2) Vulvitis, acute or chronic.

s. *Major abnormalities and defects of the genitalia* such as a change of sex, a history thereof, or complications (adhesions, disfiguring scars, etc.) residual to surgical correction of these conditions.

2-15. Urinary System
(See paras 2-8, 2-40, and 2-41.)

The causes for rejection for appointment, enlistment, and induction are—

a. *Albuminuria* if persistent or recurrent including so-called orthostatic or functional albuminuria.

b. *Cystitis, chronic.* Individuals with acute cystitis are unacceptable until the condition is cured.

c. *Enuresis* determined to be a symptom of an organic defect not amenable to treatment. (See also para 2-34.1c.)

d. *Epispadias or hypospadias* when accompanied by evidence of infection of the urinary tract or if clothing is soiled when voiding.

e. *Hematuria, cylindruria*, or other findings indicative of renal tract disease.

f. *Incontinence* of urine.

g. *Kidney*.

(1) Absence of one kidney, regardless of cause.

(2) Acute or chronic infections of the kidney.

(3) Cystic or polycystic kidney, confirmed history of.

(4) Hydronephrosis or pyonephrosis.

(5) Nephritis, acute or chronic.

(6) Pyelitis, pyelonephritis.

h. *Penis*, amputation of, if the resulting stump is insufficient to permit micturition in a normal manner.

i. *Peyronie's disease*.

j. *Prostate gland*, hypertrophy of, with urinary retention.

k. *Renal calculus*.

(1) Substantiated history of bilateral renal calculus at any time.

(2) Verified history of renal calculus at any time with evidence of stone formation within the preceding 12 months, current symptoms or positive X-ray for calculus.

l. *Skeneitis*.

m. *Urethra*.

(1) Stricture of the urethra.

(2) Urethritis, acute or chronic, other than gonorrheal urethritis without complications.

n. *Urinary fistula*.

o. *Other diseases and defects of the urinary system* which obviously preclude satisfactory performance of duty or which require frequent and prolonged treatment.

Section X. HEAD AND NECK

2-16. Head

The causes for rejection for appointment, enlistment, and induction are—

a. *Abnormalities* which are apparently temporary in character resulting from recent injuries until a period of 3 months has elapsed. These include severe contusions and other wounds of the scalp and cerebral concussion. See paragraph 2-31.

b. *Deformities of the skull* in the nature of depressions, exostoses, etc., of a degree which would prevent the individual from wearing a protective mask or military headgear.

c. *Deformities of the skull of any degree* associated with evidence of disease of the brain, spinal cord, or peripheral nerves.

d. *Depressed fractures near central sulcus* with or without convulsive seizures.

e. *Loss or congenital absence* of the bony substance of the skull not successfully corrected by reconstructive material:

(1) All cases involving absence of the bony substance of the skull which have been corrected but in which the defect is in excess of 1 square inch or the size of a 25-cent piece, will be referred to the Commander, United States Army Health Services Command together with a report of consultation;

2-9

231

(2) The report of consultation will include an evaluation of any evidence of alteration of brain function in any of its several spheres; i.e., intelligence, judgment, perception, behavior, motor control and sensory function as well as any evidence of active bone disease or other related complications. Current X-rays and other pertinent laboratory data will accompany such a report of consultation.

f. Unsightly deformities, such as large birthmarks, large hairy moles, extensive scars, and mutilations due to injuries or surgical operations; ulcerations; fistulae, atrophy, or paralysis of part of the face or head.

2–17. Neck

The causes for rejection for appointment, enlistment, and induction are—

a. Cervical ribs if symptomatic, or so obvious

that they are found on routine physical examination. (Detection based primarily on X-ray is not considered to meet this criterion.)

b. Congenital cysts of branchial cleft origin or those developing from the remnants of the thyroglossal duct, with or without fistulous tracts.

c. Fistula, chronic draining, of any type.

d. (Deleted)

e. Nonspastic contraction of the muscles of the neck or cicatricial contracture of the neck to the extent that it interferes with the wearing of a uniform or military equipment or so disfiguring as to make the individual objectionable in common social relationships.

f. Spastic contraction of the muscles of the neck, persistent, and chronic.

g. Tumor of thyroid or other structures of the neck. See paragraphs 2–40 and 2–41.

Section XI. HEART AND VASCULAR SYSTEM

2–18. Heart

The causes for rejection for appointment, enlistment, and induction are—

a. All organic valvular diseases of the heart, including those improved by surgical procedures.

b. Coronary artery disease or myocardial infarction, old or recent or true angina pectoris, at any time.

c. Electrocardiographic evidence of major arrhythmias such as—

(1) Atrial tachycardia, flutter, or fibrillation, ventricular tachycardia or fibrillation.

(2) Conduction defects such as first degree atrioventricular block and right bundle branch block. (These conditions occurring as isolated findings are not unfitting when cardiac evaluation reveals no cardiac disease.)

(3) Left bundle branch block, 2d and 3d degree AV block.

(4) Unequivocal electrocardiographic evidence of old or recent myocardial infarction; coronary insufficiency at rest or after stress; or evidence of heart muscle disease.

d. Hypertrophy or dilatation of the heart as evidenced by clinical examination or roentgenographic examination and supported by

electrocardiographic examination. Care should be taken to distinguish abnormal enlargement from increased diastolic filling as seen in the well conditioned subject with a sinus bradycardia. Cases of enlarged heart by X-ray not supported by electrocardiographic examination will be forwarded to the Commander, United States Army Health Services Command for evaluation.

e. Myocardial insufficiency (congestive circulatory failure, cardiac decompensation) obvious or covert, regardless of cause.

f. Paroxysmal tachycardia within the preceding 5 years, or at any time if recurrent or disabling or if associated with electrocardiographic evidence of accelerated A-V conduction (Wolff-Parkinson-White).

g. Pericarditis; endocarditis; or myocarditis, history or finding of, except for a history of a single acute idiopathic or coxsackie pericarditis with no residuals, or tuberculous pericarditis adequately treated with no residuals and inactive for 2 years.

h. Tachycardia persistent with a resting pulse rate of 100 or more, regardless of cause.

2–19. Vascular System

The causes for rejection for appointment, enlistment, and induction are—

2–10

232

a. *Congenital or acquired lesions of the aorta and major vessels*, such as syphilitic aortitis, demonstrable atherosclerosis which interferes with circulation, congenital or acquired dilatation of the aorta (especially if associated with other features of Marfan's syndrome), and pronounced dilatation of the main pulmonary artery.

b. *Hypertension* evidenced by preponderant diastolic blood pressure over 90-mm or preponderant systolic blood pressure over 159 at any age.

c. *Marked circulatory instability* as indicated by orthostatic hypotension, persistent tachycardia, severe peripheral vasomotor disturbances, and sympatheticotonia.

d. *Peripheral vascular disease* including Raynaud's phenomenon, Buerger's disease (thromboangiitis obliterans), erythromelalgia, arteriosclerotic, and diabetic vascular diseases. Special tests will be employed in doubtful cases.

e. *Thrombophlebitis.*

(1) History of thrombophlebitis with persistent thrombus or evidence of circulatory obstruction or deep venous incompetence in the involved veins.

(2) Recurrent thrombophlebitis.

f. *Varicose veins*, if more than mild, or if associated with edema, skin ulceration, or residual scars from ulceration.

2-20. Miscellaneous

The causes for rejection for apointment, enlistment, and induction are—

a. *Aneurysm of the heart or major vessel,* congenital or acquired.

b. *History and evidence of a congenital abnormality* which has been treated by surgery but with residual abnormalities or complications; for example: Patent ductus arteriosus with residual cardiac enlargement or pulmonary hypertension; resection of a coarctation of the aorta without a graft when there are other cardiac abnormalities or complications; closure of a secundum type atrial septal defect when there are residual abnormalities or complications.

c. *Major congenital abnormalities and defects by the heart and vessels* unless satisfactorily corrected without residuals or complications. Uncomplicated dextrocardia and other minor asymptomatic anomalies are acceptable.

d. *Substantiated history of rheumatic fever or chorea* within the previous 2 years, recurrent attacks of rheumatic fever or chorea at any time, or with evidence of residual cardiac damage.

Section XII. HEIGHT, WEIGHT, AND BODY BUILD

2-21. Height

The causes for rejection for appointment, enlistment, and induction are—

a. *For appointment.*

(1) *Men.* Height below 60 inches or over 80 inches (see administrative criteria in para 7-13).

(2) *Women.* Height below 58 inches or over 72 inches.

b. *For enlistments and induction.*

(1) *Men.* Height below 60 inches or over 80 inches for Army and Air Force.

(2) *Men.* Height below 60 inches and over 78 inches for Navy and Marine Corps.

(3) *Women.* Height below 58 inches or over 72 inches for Army.

2-22. Weight

The causes for rejection for appointment, enlistment, and induction are—

a. *Weight related to height* which is below the minimum shown in table I, appendix III for men and table II, appendix III for women.

b. *Weight related to age and height* which is in excess of the maximum shown in table I, appendix III for men and table II, appendix III for women.

2-23. Body Build

The causes for rejection for appointment, enlistment, and induction are—

a. *Congenital malformation of bones and joints.* (See paras 2-9, 2-10, and 2-11.)

b. *Deficient muscular development* which would interfere with the completion of required training.

c. *Evidences of congenital asthenia* (slender bones; weak thorax; visceroptosis; severe, chronic constipation; or "drop heart" if marked in degree).

2-11

233

d. Obesity. Even though the individual's weight is within the maximum shown in table I or II, as appropriate, appendix III, he will be reported as medically unacceptable when the medical examiner considers that the individual's weight, in relation to the bony structure and musculature, constitutes obesity of such a degree as to interfere with the satisfactory completion of prescribed training.

Section XIII. LUNGS AND CHEST WALL

2-24. General

The following conditions are causes for rejection for appointment, enlistment, and induction until further study indicates recovery without disqualifying sequelae:

a. Abnormal elevation of the diaphragm on either side.

b. Acute abscess of the lung.

c. Acute bronchitis until the condition is cured.

d. Acute fibrinous pleurisy, associated with acute nontuberculous pulmonary infection.

e. Acute mycotic disease of the lung such as coccidioidomycosis and histoplasmosis.

f. Acute nontuberculous pneumonia.

g. Foreign body in trachea or bronchus.

h. Foreign body of the chest wall causing symptoms.

i. Lobectomy, history of, for a nontuberculous nonmalignant lesion with residual pulmonary disease. Removal of more than one lobe is cause for rejection regardless of the absence of residuals.

j. Other traumatic lesions of the chest or its contents.

k. Pneumothorax or history thereof within 1 year of date of examination if due to simple trauma or surgery; within 3 years of date of examination if of spontaneous origin. Surgical correction is acceptable if no significant residual disease or deformity remains and pulmonary function tests are within normal limits.

l. Recent fracture of ribs, sternum, clavicle, or scapula.

m. Significant abnormal findings on physical examination of the chest.

2-25. Tuberculous Lesions
(See para 2-38.)

The causes for rejection for appointment, enlistment, and induction are—

a. Tuberculosis, active at any time within the past 2 years, in any form or location. A positive tuberculin skin test without other evidence of active disease is not disqualifying. Individuals taking prophylactic chemotherapy because of recent skin test conversion are not disqualified.

b. **Rescinded.**

c. Substantiated history of one or more reactivations or relapses of pulmonary tuberculosis, or other definite evidence of poor host resistance to the tubercle bacillus.

2-26. Nontuberculous Lesions

The causes for rejection for appointment, enlistment, and induction are—

a. Acute mastitis, chronic cystic mastitis, if more than mild.

b. Bronchial asthma, except for childhood asthma with a trustworthy history of freedom from symptoms since the 12th birthday.

c. Bronchitis, chronic with evidence of pulmonary function disturbance.

d. Bronchiectasis.

e. Bronchopleural fistula.

f. Bullous or generalized pulmonary emphysema.

g. Chronic abscess of lung.

h. Chronic fibrus pleuritis of sufficient extent to interfere with pulmonary function or obscure the lung field in the roentgenogram.

i. Chronic mycotic diseases of the lung including coccidioidomycosis; residual cavitation or more than a few small-sized inactive and stable residual nodules demonstrated to be due to mycotic disease.

j. Empyema, residual sacculation or unhealed sinuses of chest wall following operation for empyema.

k. Extensive pulmonary fibrosis from any cause, producing dyspnea or exertion.

l. Foreign body of the lung or mediastinum causing symptoms or active inflammatory reaction.

2-12

234

m. Multiple cystic disease of the lung or solitary cyst which is large and incapacitating.

n. New growth of breast; history of mastectomy.

o. Osteomyelitis of rib, sternum, clavicle, scapula, or vertebra.

p. Pleurisy with effusion of unknown origin within the previous 2 years.

q. Sarcoidosis. See paragraph 2–38.

r. Suppurative periostitis of rib, sternum, clavicle, scapula, or vertebra.

Section XIV. MOUTH, NOSE, PHARYNX, TRACHEA, ESOPHAGUS, AND LARYNX

2–27. Mouth

The causes for rejection for appointment, enlistment, and induction are—

a. *Hard palate*, perforation of.

b. *Harelip*, unless satisfactorily repaired by surgery.

c. *Leukoplakia*, if severe.

d. *Lips*, unsightly mutilations of, from wounds, burns, or disease.

e. *Ranula*, if extensive. For other tumors see paragraphs 2–40 and 2–41.

2–28. Nose

The causes for rejection of appointment, enlistment, and induction are—

a. *Allergic manifestations.*

(1) Chronic atrophic rhinitis.

(2) Hay fever if severe; and if not controllable by antihistamines or by desensitization, or both.

b. *Choana, atresia, or stenosis* of, if symptomatic.

c. *Nasal septum,* perforation of:

(1) Associated with the interference of function, ulceration or crusting, and when the result of organic disease.

(2) If progressive.

(3) If respiration is accompanied by a whistling sound.

d. *Sinusitis,* acute.

e. *Sinusitis,* chronic, when more than mild:

(1) Evidenced by any of the following: Chronic purulent nasal discharge, large nasal polyps, hyperplastic changes of the nasal tissues, or symptoms requiring frequent medical attention.

(2) Confirmed by transillumination of X-ray examination or both.

2–29. Pharynx, Trachea, Esophagus, and Larynx

The causes for rejection for appointment, enlistment, and induction are—

a. *Esophagus,* organic disease of, such as ulceration, varices, achalasia; peptic esophagitis; if confirmed by appropriate X-ray or esophagoscopic examinations.

b. *Laryngeal paralysis,* sensory or motor, due to any cause.

c. *Larynx,* organic disease of, such as neoplasm, polyps, granuloma, ulceration, and chronic laryngitis.

★d. *Dysphonia plicae ventricularis.*

e. *Tracheostomy or tracheal fistula.*

2–30. Other Defects and Diseases

The causes for rejection for appointment, enlistment, and induction are—

a. *Aphonia.*

b. *Deformities or conditions of the mouth, throat, pharynx, larynx, esophagus, and nose* which interfere with mastication and swallowing of ordinary food, with speech, or with breathing.

c. *Destructive syphilitic disease of the mouth, nose, throat, larynx, or esophagus* (para 2–42).

d. *Pharyngitis and nasopharyngitis,* chronic, with positive history and objective evidence, if of such a degree as to result in excessive time lost in the military environment.

2–13

Section XV. NEUROLOGICAL DISORDERS

2-31. Neurological Disorders

The causes for rejection for appointment, enlistment, and induction are—

a. *Degenerative disorders.*
(1) Cerebellar and Friedreich's ataxia.
(2) Cerebral arteriosclerosis.
(3) Encephalomyelitis, residuals of, which preclude the satisfactory performance of military duty.
(4) Huntington's chorea.
(5) Multiple sclerosis.
(6) Muscular atrophies and dystrophies of any type.

b. *Miscellaneous.*
(1) Congenital malformations if associated with neurological manifestations and meningocele even if uncomplicated.
(2) Migraine when frequent and incapacitating.
(3) Paralysis or weakness, deformity, discoordination, pain, sensory disturbance, intellectual deficit, disturbances of consciousness, or personality abnormalities regardless of cause which is of such a nature or degree as to preclude the satisfactory performance of military duty.
(4) Tremors, spasmodic torticollis, athetosis or other abnormal movements more than mild.

c. *Neurosyphilis* of any form (general paresis, tabes dorsalis, meningovascular syphilis).

★d. *Paroxysmal convulsive disorders, disturbances of consciousness, all forms of psychomotor or temporal lobe epilepsy* or history thereof except under the following circumstances:

(1) No seizure since age 5.

(2) Individuals who have had seizures since age 5 but who, during the 5 years immediately preceding examination for military service, have been totally seizure free and have not been taking any type of anticonvulsant medication for the entire period will be considered on an individual case basis. Documentation in these cases must be from attending or consulting physicians and the original electroencephalogram tracing (not a copy) taken within the preceding 3 months must be submitted for evaluation by the Surgeon General of the service to which the individual is applying.

e. *Peripheral nerve disorder.*

(1) Polyneuritis.

(2) Mononeuritis or neuralgia which is chronic or recurrent and of an intensity that is periodically incapacitating.

(3) Neurofibromatosis.

f. *Spontaneous subarachnoid hemorrhage,* verified history of, unless cause has been surgically corrected.

★Section XVI. MENTAL DISORDERS

Diagnostic concepts and terms utilized in this section are in consonance with the Diagnostic and Statistical Manual, Third Edition (DSM–III), American Psychiatric Association, 1980.

2-32. Disorders with Psychotic Features

The causes for rejection for appointment, enlistment and induction are—
History of a mental disorder with gross impairment in reality testing. This does not include transient disorders associated with intoxication, severe stress or secondary to a toxic, infectious or other organic process.

2-33. Affective Disorders (Mood Disorders)

The causes for rejection for appointment, enlistment and induction are—
Persistence or recurrence of symptoms sufficient to cause interference with social, educational or vocational functioning or necessitate maintenance treatment or hospitalization.

2-34. Anxiety, Somatoform or Dissociative Disorders (Alternatively may be addressed as Neurotic Disorders)

The causes for rejection for appointment, enlistment and induction are—

2-14

a. History of such disorder(s) resulting in any or all of the below:

(1) Hospitalization.

(2) Prolonged care by a physician or other professional.

(3) Loss of time from normal pursuits for repeated periods even if of brief duration, or

(4) Symptoms or behavior of a repeated nature which impaired social, school or work efficiency.

b. History of an episode of such disorders within the preceding 12 months which was sufficiently severe to require professional attention or absence from work or school for more than a brief period (maximum of 7 days).

2-34.1. Personality, Behavior or Learning Disorders

The causes for rejection for appointment, enlistment and induction are—

a. Personality or behavior disorders, as evidenced by frequent encounters with law enforcement agencies, antisocial attitudes or behavior which, while not sufficient cause for administrative rejection, are tangible evidence of impaired characterological capacity to adapt to the military service

b. Personality or behavior disorders where it is evident by history interview and/or psychologic testing that the degree of immaturity, instability, personality inadequacy, impulsivity or dependency will seriously interfere with adjustment in the military service as demonstrated by repeated inability to maintain reasonable adjustment in school, with employers and fellow-workers, and other society groups.

c. Other behavior problems including but not limited to conditions such as authenticated evidence of functional enuresis, sleepwalking, which is habitual or persistent, not due to an organic condition (para 2-15c) occurring beyond early adolescence (age 12 to 14) or stammering or stuttering of such a degree that the individual is normally unable to express himself clearly or to repeat commands.

d. Specific learning defects secondary to organic or functional mental disorders sufficient to impair capacity to read and understand at a level acceptable to perform military duties.

★2-34.2. Psychosexual Conditions

The causes for rejection for appointment, enlistment and induction are—

a. Homosexual behavior. This includes all homosexual activity except adolescent experimentation or the occurrence of a single episode of homosexual behavior while intoxicated.

b. Transsexualism and other gender identity disorders.

c. Exhibitionism, transvestism, voyeurism and other paraphilias.

2-34.3. Substance Misuse

The causes for rejection for appointment, enlistment and induction are—

a. Chronic alcoholism or alcohol addiction/dependence.

b. Drug addiction or dependence.

c. Drug abuse characterized by—

(1) The evidence of use of any controlled, hallucinogenic or other intoxicating substance at time of examination when the use cannot be accounted for as the result of the advice of a recognized health care practitioner.

(2) Documented misuse or abuse of any controlled substance requiring professional care (including cannabinoids) within a 1-year period prior to examination. Cases indicating use of marijuana or other cannabinoids (not habitual use) or experimental or casual use of other drugs, except as noted in *(b)* above, may be waived by competent authority as established by the respective service if there is evidence of current drug abstinence and the individual is otherwise qualified for service.

(3) The repeated self-procurement and self-administration of any drug or chemical substance, including cannabinoids, with such frequency that it appears that the examinee has accepted the use of or reliance on these substances as part of his pattern of behavior. See also TB MED 290.

d. Alcohol abuse. The cause of rejection for appointment, enlistment and induction is the repeated use of alcoholic beverages which leads to misconduct, unacceptable social behavior, poor work or academic performance, impaired physical or mental health, lack of financial responsibility or disrupted personal relationships within 1 year of examination. See also TB MED 290.

2-15

237

Section XVII. SKIN AND CELLULAR TISSUES

2-35. Skin and Cellular Tissues

The causes for rejection for appointment, enlistment, and induction are—

a. *Acne.* Severe, when the face is markedly disfigured, or when extensive involvement of the neck, shoulders, chest, or back would be aggravated by or intefere with the wearing of military equipment.

b. *Atopic dermatitis.* With active or residual lesions in characteristic areas (face and neck, antecubital and popliteal fossae, occasionally wrists and hands), or documented history thereof.

c. *Cysts.*

(1) *Cysts, other than pilonidal.* Of such a size or location as to interfere with the normal wearing of military equipment.

(2) *Cysts, pilonidal.* Pilonidal cysts, if evidenced by the presence of a tumor mass or a discharging sinus.

d. *Dermatitis factitia.*

e. *Dermatitis herpetiformis.*

f. *Eczema.* Any type which is chronic and resistant to treatment.

f.1. *Elephantiasis or chronic lymphedema.*

g. *Epidermolysis bullosa; pemphigus.*

h. *Fungus infections,* systemic or superficial types: If extensive and not amenable to treatment.

i. *Furunculosis.* Extensive, recurrent, or chronic.

j. *Hyperhidrosis* of hands or feet. Chronic or severe.

k. *Ichthyosis.* Severe.

l. *Leprosy.* Any type.

m. *Leukemia cutis; mycosis fungoides; Hodgkin's disease.*

n. *Lichen planus.*

o. *Lupus erythematosus* (acute, subacute, or chronic) or any other dermatosis aggravated by sunlight.

p. *Neurofibromatosis* (Von Recklinghausen's disease).

q. *Nevi or vascular tumors.* If extensive, unsightly, or exposed to constant irritation.

r. *Psoriasis* or a verified history thereof.

s. *Radiodermatitis.*

t. *Scars* which are so extensive, deep, or adherent that they may interfere with the wearing of military equipment, or that show a tendency to ulcerate.

u. *Scleroderma.* Diffuse type.

v. *Tuberculosis.* See paragraph 2-38.

w. *Urticaria.* Chronic.

x. *Warts, plantar,* which have materially interfered with the following of a useful vocation in civilian life.

y. *Xanthoma.* If disabling or accompanied by hypercholesterolemia or hyperlipemia.

x. *Any other chronic skin disorder* of a degree or nature which requires frequent outpatient treatment or hospitalization, interferes with the satisfactory performance of duty, or is so disfiguring as to make the individual objectionable in ordinary social relationships.

aa. When in the opinion of the examining physician tattoos will significantly limit effective performance of military service the individual will be referred to the MEPS Commander, for final determination of acceptability.

Section XVIII. SPINE, SCAPULAE, RIBS, AND SACROILIAC JOINTS

2-36. Spine and Sacroiliac Joints
(See also para 2-11.)

The causes for rejection for appointment, enlistment, and induction are—

a. *Arthritis.* See paragraph 2-11a.

b. *Complaint of disease or injury of the spine or sacroiliac joints* either with or without objective signs which has prevented the individual from successfully following a physically active vocation in civilian life. Substantiation or documentation of the complaint without objective signs is required.

c. *Deviation or curvature of spine* from normal alignment, structure, or function (scoliosis, kyphosis, or lordosis) if—

(1) Mobility and weight-bearing power is poor.

(2) More than moderate restriction of normal physical activities is required.

2-16

(3) Of such a nature as to prevent the individual from following a *physically active vocation* in civilian life.

(4) Of a degree which will interfere with the wearing of a uniform or military equipment.

(5) Symptomatic associated with positive physical finding(s) and demonstrable by X-ray.

d. Diseases of the lumbosacral or sacroiliac joints of a chronic type and obviously associated with pain referred to the lower extremities, muscular spasm, postural deformities and limitation of motion in the lumbar region of the spine.

e. Granulomatous diseases either active or healed.

f. Healed fracture of the spine or pelvic bones with associated symptoms which have prevented the individual from following a *physically* active vocation in civilian life or which preclude the satisfactory performance of military duty.

g. Ruptured nucleus pulposus (herniation of intervertebral disk) or history of operation for this condition.

h. Spondylolysis or spondylolisthesis that is symptomatic or is likely to interfere with performance of duty or is likely to require assignment limitations.

2–37. Scapulae, Clavicles, and Ribs
(See para 2–11.)

The causes for rejection for appointment, enlistment, and induction are—

a. Fractures, until well-healed, and until determined that the residuals thereof will not preclude the satisfactory performance of military duty.

b. Injury within the preceding 6 weeks, without fracture, or dislocation, of more than a minor nature.

c. Osteomyelitis of rib, sternum, clavicle, scapula, or vertebra.

d. Prominent scapulae interfering with function or with the wearing of uniform or military equipment.

Section XIX. SYSTEMIC DISEASES AND MISCELLANEOUS CONDITIONS AND DEFECTS

2–38. Systemic Diseases

The causes for rejection for appointment, enlistment, and induction are—

a. Dermatomyositis.

b. Lupus erythematosus, acute, subacute, or chronic.

c. Progresive systemic sclerosis.

d. Reiter's disease.

e. Sarcoidosis.

f. Scleroderma, diffuse type.

g. Tuberculosis.

(1) Active tuberculosis in any form or location or substantiated history of active tuberculosis within the previous 2 years.

(2) Substantiated history of one or more reactivations or relapses of tuberculosis in any form or location or other definite evidence of poor host resistance to the tubercle bacillus.

(3) Residual physical or mental defects from past tuberculosis that would preclude the satisfactory performance of duty.

2–39. General and Miscellaneous Conditions and Defects

The causes for rejection for appointment, enlistment, and induction are—

a. Allergic manifestations.

(1) Allergic rhinitis (hay fever). See paragraph 2–28.

(2) Asthma. See paragraph 2–26*b*.

(3) Allergic dermatoses. See paragraph 2–35.

(4) Visceral, abdominal, and cerebral allergy, if severe or not responsive to treatment.

(5) Bona fide history of moderate or severe generalized (as opposed to local) allergic reaction to insect bites or stings. Bona fide history of severe generalized reaction to common foods; e.g., milk, eggs, beef, and pork.

b. Any acute pathological condition, including acute communicable diseases, until recovery has occurred without sequelae.

c. Any deformity which is markedly unsightly or which impairs general functional ability to such an extent as to prevent satisfactory performance of military duty.

d. Chronic metallic poisoning especially beryllium, manganese, and mercury. Undesirable

2–17

residuals from lead, arsenic, or silver poisoning make the examinee medically unacceptable.

e. *Cold injury,* residuals of (*example:* frostbite, chilblain, immersion foot, or trench foot), such as deep-seated ache, paresthesia, hyperhidrosis, easily traumatized skin, cyanosis, amputation of any digit, or ankylosis.

f. *Reactive tests for syphilis* such as the RPR or VDRL followed by a reactive, confirmatory Fluorescent Treponemal Antibody Absorption (FTA-ABS) test unless there is a documented history of adequately treated syphilis. In the absence of clinical findings, the presence of a reactive RPR or VDRL followed by a negative FTA-ABS test is not disqualifying if a cause for the false positive reaction can be identified or if the test reverts to a nonreactive status during an appropriate followup period (3–6 months).

g. *Filariasis; trypanosomiasis; amebiasis; schistosomiasis; uncinariasis* (hookworm) asso-

ciated with anemia, malnutrition, etc., if more than mild, and other similar worm or animal parasitic infestations, including the carrier states thereof.

h. *Heat pyrexia* (heatstroke, sunstroke, etc.): Documented evidence of predisposition (includes disorders of sweat mechanism and previous serious episode), recurrent episode requiring medical attention, or residual injury resulting therefrom (especially cardiac, cerebral, hepatic, and renal).

i. *Industrial solvent* and other chemical intoxication, chronic including carbon bisulfide, tricholorethylene, carbon tetrachloride, and methyl cellosolve.

j. *Mycotic infection* of internal organs.

k. *Myositis or fibrositis;* severe, chronic.

l. *Residual of tropical fevers* and various parasitic or protozoal infestations which in the opinion of the medical examiner preclude the satisfactory performance of military duty.

Section XX. TUMORS AND MALIGNANT DISEASES

2–40. Benign Tumors

The causes for rejetion for appointment, enlistment, and induction are—

a. *Any tumor of the*—
(1) Auditory canal, if obstructive.
(2) Eye or orbit, (para 2–12a(6)).
(3) Kidney, bladder, testicle, or penis.
(4) Central nervous system and its membranous coverings unless 5 years after surgery and no otherwise disqualifying residuals of surgery or of original lesion.

b. *Benign tumors of the abdominal wall* if sufficiently large to interfere with miliary duty.

c. *Benign tumors of the bone* likely to continue to enlarge, be subjected to trauma during military service, or show malignant potential.

d. *Benign tumors of the thyroid* or other structures of the neck, including enlarged lymph nodes, if the enlargment is of such degree as to

interfere with the wearing of a uniform or military equipment.

e. *Tongue, benign tumor of,* if it interferes with function.

f. *Breast, thoracic contents, or chest wall,* tumors of, other than fibromata lipomata, and inclusion or sebaceous cysts which do not interfere with military duty.

g. *For tumors of the internal or external female genitalia* see paragraph 2–14h.

2–41. Malignant Diseases and Tumors

The causes for rejection for appointment, enlistment, and induction are—

a. *Leukemia,* acute or chronic.

b. *Malignant lymphomata.*

c. *Malignant tumor,* except for small early basal cell epitheliomas, at any time, even though surgically removed, confirmed by accepted laboratory procedures.

Section XXI. VENEREAL DISEASES

2–42. Venereal Diseases

In general the finding of acute, uncomplicated venereal disease which can be expected to re-

spond to treatment is not a cause for medical rejection for military service. The causes for rejection for appointment, enlistment, and induction

2-18

are—

a. Chronic venereal disease which has not satisfactorily responded to treatment. The finding of a positive serologic test for syphilis following the adequate treatment of syphilis is not in itself considered evidence of chronic venereal disease which has not responded to treatment (para 2–39*f*).

b. Complications and permanent residuals of venereal disease if progressive, of such nature as to interfere with the satisfactory performance of duty, or if subject to aggravation by military service.

c. Neurosyphilis. See paragraph 2–31*c*.

★APPENDIX II
TABLES OF ACCEPTABLE AUDIOMETRIC HEARING LEVEL

Hearing of all applicants for appointment, enlistment or induction will be tested by audiometers calibrated to the International Standards Organization (ISO 1964) and the American National Standards Institute (ANSI 1969).

All audiometric tracings or audiometric readings recorded on reports of medical examination or other medical records will be clearly identified.

Table I. Acceptable Audiometric Hearing Level for Appointment, Enlistment and Induction
ISO 1964—ANSI 1969

Frequency	*Both ears*
500 Hz	Audiometer average level of 6 readings (3 per ear) at 500, 1000 and 2000 Hz
1000 Hz	not more than 30 dB, with no individual level greater than 35 dB at these
2000 Hz	frequencies, and level not more than 55 dB each ear at 4000 Hz; or audiome-
4000 Hz	ter level 30 dB at 500 Hz, 25 dB at 1000 and 2000 Hz, and 35 dB at 4000 Hz in the better ear.

OR

If the average of the 3 speech frequencies is greater than 30 dB ISO–ANSI, reevaluate the better ear only in accordance with the following table of acceptability:

Frequency	*Better ear*
500 Hz	30 dB
1000 Hz	25 dB
2000 Hz	25 dB
4000 Hz	35 dB

The poorer ear may be deaf.

Table II. Acceptable Audiometric Hearing Level for Army Aviation, Including Air Traffic Controllers
ISO 1964—ANSI 1969 (Unaided Sensitivity)

Frequency		500Hz	1000Hz	2000Hz	3000Hz	4000Hz	6000Hz
Classes 1 & 1A	Each ear	25dB	25dB	25dB	35dB	45dB	45dB
Class 2	Better ear	25dB	25dB	25dB	35dB	65dB	75dB
(Aviators)	Poorer ear	25dB	35db	35dB	45dB	65dB	75dB
Class 2 (Air Traffic Controllers)	Each ear	25dB	25dB	25dB	35dB	65dB	75dB
Class 3	Better ear	25dB	25dB	25dB	35dB	65dB	75dB
	Poorer ear	25dB	35dB	35dB	45dB	65dB	75dB

Table III. Acceptable Audiometric Hearing Level for Admission to US Military Academy, Uniformed Services University of Health Sciences, and Army ROTC Scholarship Program
ISO 1964—ANSI 1969 (Unaided Sensitivity)

Frequency	500Hz	1000Hz	2000Hz	3000Hz	4000Hz	6000Hz
Each ear	25dB	25dB	25dB	45dB	45dB	45dB

APPENDIX III
TABLES OF WEIGHT

Table 1. Table of Militarily Acceptable Weight (in Pounds) as Related to Age and Height for Males—Initial Procurement

Height (inches)	Minimum (regardless of age)	*MAXIMUM				
		16–20 years	21–30 years	31–35 years	36–40 years	41 years and over
60	100	158	163	162	157	150
61	102	163	168	167	162	155
62	103	168	174	173	168	160
63	104	174	180	178	173	165
64	105	179	185	184	179	171
65	106	185	191	190	184	176
66	107	191	197	196	190	182
67	111	197	203	202	196	187
68	115	203	209	208	202	193
69	119	209	215	214	208	198
70	123	215	222	220	214	204
71	127	221	228	227	220	210
72	131	227	234	233	226	216
73	135	233	241	240	233	222
74	139	240	248	246	239	228
75	143	246	254	253	246	234
76	147	253	261	260	252	241
77	151	260	268	266	259	247
78	153	267	275	273	266	254
*79	159	273	282	281	273	260
*80	166	280	289	288	279	267

*Applies only to personnel enlisted, inducted, or appointed in the Army and enlisted or inducted into the Air Force. Does not apply to Navy or Marine Corps enlistees or inductees.

★Table II. Table of Militarily Acceptable Weight (in Pounds) as Related to Age and Height for Females—Initial Procurement

Height (inches)	Minimum (regardless of age)	Maximum					
		18–20 yrs	21–24 yrs	25–30 yrs	31–35 yrs	36–40 yrs	41 yrs and over
58	90	120	124	126	129	132	135
59	92	122	126	128	131	134	137
60	94	124	128	130	133	136	139
61	96	127	130	132	135	139	141
62	98	128	132	134	137	140	144
63	100	132	134	136	139	143	145
64	102	135	136	139	143	145	149
65	104	138	140	144	148	150	153
66	106	141	145	148	151	154	157
67	109	145	149	152	156	158	162
68	112	150	153	156	160	162	166
69	115	154	157	161	164	167	170
70	118	158	162	165	168	171	174
71	122	162	166	169	173	175	179
72	125	167	171	174	178	181	184
73	128	171	177	179	183	186	190
74	130	175	182	185	188	191	195
75	133	179	187	190	194	196	200
76	136	184	192	196	199	202	205
77	139	188	197	201	204	207	211
78	141	192	203	206	209	213	216
79	144	196	208	211	215	218	220
80	147	201	213	216	219	223	225

★Table III. Table of Acceptable Weights for Army Aviation
(Classes 1, 1A, 2, 3) (Rescinded)
See AR 600–9, The Army Weight Control Program.

★Table IV. Table of Acceptable Weight (In Pounds) as Related to Height for Diving Duty.
(Rescinded)
See AR 600–9, The Army Weight Control Program.

D. FOOTNOTES

Abbreviations

```
========================================================
```

AR = Army Regulation
CFR = Code of Federal Regulation
DoD Dir. = Department of Defense Directive
MEPCOM Reg. = Military Enlistment Processing
                   Command Regulation
P.L. = Public Law
Prec. Proc. = Presidential Proclamation
Reg. = Selective Service regulations
      (32 CFR Secs. 1600 et seq.)
RIMS = Registrant Informations Management System
SSLR = Selective Service Law Reporter
USC = United States Code

```
========================================================
```

Chapter 1: HOW THE DRAFT SYSTEM WORKS
1. 50 USC App. Sec. 451 et seq.
2. Reg. Secs. 1633.2(c); 1633.1(f)
3. Reg. Sec. 1609.1
4. Reg. Sec. 1605.51
5. Reg. Sec. 1609.3
6. Reg. Secs. 1633.2(b); 1633.1(e)
7. Reg. Sec. 1605.21
8. Reg. Secs. 1605.22; 1609.1
9. Reg. Sec. 1602.16; MEPCOM Reg. 40-1
10. Reg. Sec. 1630.44
11. 50 USC App. Sec. 467(c)
12. Reg. Sec. 1618.1
13. Reg. Seg. 1618.1

Chapter 3: REGISTRATION AND RESISTANCE
1. 50 USC App. Sec. 463
2. 50 USC App. Sec. 453
3. 50 USC App. Sec. 462
4. 50 USC App. Sec. 462
5. 18 USC Sec. 3282
6. 50 USC App. Sec. 462(d)
7. 18 USC Sec. 3290

8. U.S. v. Grady, 544 F. 2d 598 (2nd Cir. 1976)
9. 50 USC App. 462(d)
10. U.S. v. Baechler, 509 F. 2d 13 (4th Cir. 1974); U.S. v. Cannon, 181 F. 2d 354 (9 Cir. 1950); U.S. v. Houseman, 335 F. Supp. 226 (SD-NY 1971)
11. Pres. Proc. 4771 (1980)
12. Reg. Secs. 1633.3; 1636.2
13. Reg. Sec. 1621.1(a)

Chapter 4: THE DRAFT LOTTERY
1. Reg. Sec. 1624.4
2. Reg. Sec. 1624.4
3. Reg. Sec. 1624.4(e); c.f. 1624.3(c)
4. Reg. Sec. 1624.1(b)
5. Reg. Sec. 1624.4(c)
6. Reg. Sec. 1624.7
7. Reg. Sec. 1624.4(b)

Chapter 5: INDUCTION
1. Reg. Sec. 1632.2(h)
2. Reg. Sec. 1624.6(a)
3. Reg. Sec. 1633.44(a)
4. Reg. Sec. 1624.9
5. Reg. Sec. 1624.6(c)
6. Reg. Sec. 1624.5(a)
7. Reg. Sec. 1624.4
8. Reg. Sec. 1633.2(i)
9. Reg. Sec. 1624.6
10. Reg. Sec. 1624.5(c)

11. DoD Dir. 1300.6
12. Disposition of Defendants, 1944-1970, SSLR 6001-6005

Chapter 6: CLASSIFICATION
1. Reg. Sec. 1630.10(b)
2. Reg. Sec. 1633.3
3. Reg. Sec. 1618.1
4. Reg. Secs. 1633.2(h); 1633.4
5. Reg. Sec. 1633.11
6. Reg. Sec. 1648.3(a)
7. Reg. Sec. 1648.3(b)
8. Reg. Sec. 1633.2(b)
9. Reg. Sec. 1648.3(c)
10. Reg. Sec. 1633.6

Chapter 7: CONSCIENTIOUS OBJECTION
1. U.S. v. MacIntosh, 283 US 605, 624 (1931)
2. 50 USC App. Sec. 456(j)
3. Clay v. US, 403 US 698 (1971)
4. Reg. Sec. 1656.2
5. Reg. Sec. 1633.6
6. Reg. Sec. 1630.17
7. Reg. Sec. 1656.2
8. Reg. Sec. 1656.5(e)
9. US v. Seeger, 380 US 163 (1965); Welsh v. US, 398 US 33 (1970)
10. Clay v. US, supra.
11. Gilette v. US, 401 US 437 (1971)

12. Fleming v. US, 344 F.2d 912 (10th Cir. 1965)
13. Sicurella v. US, 348 US 385 (1955)
14. Ehlert v. US, 402 US 99 (1971)
15. Reg. Sec. 1633.3
16. Reg. Sec. 1633.2(h)
17. Reg. Sec. 1618.1
18. Reg. Sec. 1621.1(c)
19. Reg. Sec. 1656.10(b)
20. Reg. Sec. 1656.5
21. Reg. Sec. 1656.2
22. Gibson, Dodez v. US, 329 US 338 (1946); Reg. Sec. 1656.11(c)
23. Reg. Sec. 1656.14
24. Reg. Sec. 1656.11(b)(3)
25. Reg. Secs. 1656.1(b)(14); 1656.5
26. Reg. Sec. 1656.12(a)(1)
27. Reg. Sec. 1656.12(a)(2)
28. Reg. Sec. 1656.12(a)(6)
29. Reg. Sec. 1656.13
30. Reg. Sec. 1656.13(d)
31. Reg. Sec. 1656.13(h)(2)
32. Reg. Sec. 1656.15
33. Reg. Sec. 1624.7
34. See, e.g., AR 635-200, Ch. 6
35. Reg. Secs. 1656.16(b)(1); 1656.16(b)(2)
36. Reg. Sec. 1656.16(b)(3)
37. Reg. Sec. 1656.16(b)(4)
38. Reg. Sec. 1630.18
39. Reg. Sec. 1656.19(b)
40. Reg. Sec. 1648.3(a)
41. Reg. Sec. 1648.4(b)
42. Lockhart v. US, 420 F.2d 1143 (1969)
43. Reg. Sec. 1633.12
44. Reg. Sec. 1633.2(i)
45. Disposition of Defendants, 1944-1970, SSLR 6001-6005

Chapter 8: DEPENDENCY DEFERMENTS
1. Reg. Sec. 1630.30
2. Reg. Sec. 1642.1(b)(1)
3. Reg. Sec. 1642.3(a)(1)
4. Reg. Sec. 1642.3
5. Reg. Sec. 1648.3(b)
6. Reg. Sec. 1648.4(c)
7. Reg. Sec. 1642.7(a)
8. Reg. Sec. 1642.4(b)

Chapter 9: SURVIVING SONS
1. McKart v. US, 395 US 185 (1969)
2. Reg. Sec. 1630.45
3. P.L. 92-129, Sec.101(d)(3)
4. McKart v. US, supra.
5. 50 USC App. Sec. 456(o)(1)
6. 50 USC App. Sec. 456(o)(2)
7. 50 USC App. Sec. 456(o)
8. McKart v. US, supra.

Chapter 10: MINISTERS
1. Reg. Sec. 1630.43
2. Reg. Sec. 1630.26
3. 50 USC App. Sec. 466(g)
4. 50 USC App. Sec. 466(g)(3)
5. Dickinson v. US, 346 US 389 (1953)
6. US v. Pryor, 488 F.2d 1273 (9th Cir. 1971)
7. 50 USC App. Sec. 466(g)
8. Reg. Sec. 1639.3(a)
9. Reg. Secs. 1602.13; 1633.1(d)
10. Reg. Sec. 1648.3(b)
11. Reg. Sec. 1648.4(c)

Chapter 11: MISCELLANEOUS CLASSIFICATIONS
1. Reg. Sec. 1633.2(b)
2. Reg. Sec. 1633.2(d)
3. Reg. Sec. 1630.13
4. Reg. Sec. 1630.14
5. Reg. Sec. 1630.12
6. Reg. Sec. 1630.40
7. Reg. Sec. 1630.41
8. Reg. Sec. 1633.2(a)
9. Reg. Sec. 1630.15

Chapter 12: THE MEDICAL EXAMINATION
1. Reg. Sec. 1630.44
2. MEPCOM Reg. 40-1
3. AR 40-501, Chapters 2, 6, 8
4. Reg. Sec. 1630.44(a)
5. AR 40-501, Chapter 1, Par. 1-2(a)
6. Reg. Sec. 1624.10

Chapter 13: GAYS AND THE DRAFT
1. Diagnostic Statistical Manual, III
2. AR 40-501, Ch. 2, para. 2-34.2 a
3. U.S. v. Anderson, 5SSLR 3843 (9th Cir. 1972)
4. U.S. v. Houseman, Supra
5. AR 40-501, Ch. 2, para. 2-34.2 a
6. 5 USC Sec. 552a; 50 USC App. Sec. 462(a); Reg. Sec. 1609.7

Chapter 14: DISAGREEABLE CLASSIFICATION
1. Reg. Sec. 1633.1(d)
2. Reg. Sec. 1633.1(f)
3. Reg. Secs. 1633.1(b); 1633.1(e)
4. Reg. Sec. 1633.2(b)
5. Reg. Secs. 1624.6(a); 1624.6(h)
6. Reg. Sec. 1633.2(b)
7. RIMS Manual Sec. 9.11
8. Reg. Sec. 1633.1(f)
9. Reg. Sec. 1630.44

10. Rec. Sec. 1633.1(e)
11. Rec. Sec. 1651.1(b)
12. Rec. Sec. 1653.1(b)
13. Rec. Sec. 1633.1(d)
14. Rec. Sec. 1648.3(a)
15. Rec. Sec. 1648.3(b)
16. Rec. Sec. 1651.1(b)
17. Rec. Sec. 1653.1(b)
18. Rec. Sec. 1618.1
19. Rec. Sec. 1651.2
20. Rec. Sec. 1651.4(e)
21. Rec. Sec. 1618.2
22. 5 USC Sec. 552a
23. Reingehl v. Hershey, 426 F. 2d 815 (9th Cir. 1970)

Chapter 15: LOCAL BOARD PERSONAL APPEARANCE

1. Reg. Sec. 1648.3
2. Reg. Sec. 1648.3(a)
3. Reg. Secs. 1648.3(b); 1648.3(c)
4. Reg. Sec. 1618.1
5. Reg. Sec. 1648.4(a)
6. Reg. Sec. 1633.1(e)
7. 50 USC App. Sec. 462(a)
8. Reg. Sec. 1621.1(b)
9. Reg. Sec. 1633.11
10. Reg. Sec. 1648.2(a)
11. Reg. Sec. 1648.2(b)
12. Reg. Sec. 1648.2(d)
13. Reg. Sec. 1621.1(a)
14. Reg. Sec. 1648.5(c)
15. Reg. Sec. 1648.5(b)
16. Reg. Sec. 1648.5(f)

17. Reg. Sec. 1648.5(g)
18. Reg. Sec. 1648.5(e)
19. Reg. Sec. 1648.5(i)
20. Reg. Sec. 1648.5(a)
21. Reg. Sec. 1648.5(c)
22. Reg. Sec. 1648.5(f)
23. Reg. Sec. 1648.5(g)
24. Reg. Sec. 1648.5(h)
25. Reg. Sec. 1648.5(d)
26. Reg. Sec. 1651.2
27. Reg. Secs. 1651.3(c); 1651.4(g)
28. Reg. Sec. 1651.4(g)
29. Reg. Sec. 1651.4(e)
30. Reg. Sec. 1651.4(e)

Chapter 16: THE DISTRICT APPEAL

1. Reg. Sec. 1651.2
2. Reg. Sec. 1651.3(c)
3. Reg. Sec. 1651.4(g)
4. Reg. Sec. 1651.4(k)
5. Reg. Sec. 1651.3(b)
6. Reg. Sec. 1633.9
7. Reg. Sec. 1633.9
8. Reg. Sec. 1633.8
9. Reg. Sec. 1636.6(a)
10. U.S. v. Hayden, 445 F. 2d 1365 (9th Cir. 1971)
11. Reg. Secs. 1651.2; 1602.9
12. Reg. Sec. 1651.4(f)
13. Reg. Sec. 1651.4(i)
14. Reg. Secs. 1633.9; 1633.10
15. Reg. Sec. 1653.1(b)
16. Reg. Sec. 1653.1(b)

17. Reg. Sec. 1633.2(i)

Chapter 17: DRAFT CASES IN COURT
1. 50 USC App. Sec. 460(b)(3)
2. 50 USC App. Sec. 462(a)
3. Dickinson v. US, 346 US 389 (1953)
4. Reg. Sec. 1636.10
5. US v. Haughton, 413 F.2d 736 (9th Cir. 1969)
6. US v. Hayden, 445 F.2d 1365 (9th Cir. 1971)
7. Ibid.
8. US v. Andersen, 447 F.2d 1063 (9th Cir. 1971)
9. US v. Atherton, 430 F.2d 741 (9th Cir. 1970)
10. Falbo v. US, 320 US 549 (1944)
11. For example: Arver v. US, 245 US 366 (1918); US v. Thomason, 444 F.2d 1094 (9th Cir. 1971); US v. Zaugh, 445 F.2d 300 (9th Cir. 1971); US v. Burns, 446 F.2d 896 (9th Cir. 1971); US v. Lumsden, 449 F.2d 154 (9th Cir. 1971)
12. Disposition of Defendants, 1944–1970, SSLR 6019
13. Ibid.
14. 18 USC Secs. 5005 et. seq.

Appendix A: ALIENS AND THE DRAFT
1. 50 USC App. Secs. 453, 456(a); 8 USC Sec. 1101(a)(15)
2. 50 USC App. Sec. 453
3. Reg. Sec. 1621.1
4. 50 USC App. Sec. 455(a)(3); Reg. Sec. 1630.42(e)
5. 8 USC Sec. 1448
6. Reg. Sec. 1648.5(e)
7. 8 USC Sec. 1182(a)(15)
8. 8 USC Sec. 1182(a)
9. 8 USC Sec. 1182(a)(4)
10. Lesbian & Gay Freedom Day Committee v. U.S.I.N.S., 541 F. Supp. 569 (ND-Cal. 1982)
11. Reg. Sec. 1630.42(b)
12. 8 USC Sec. 1182(a)(22)
13 Reg. Sec. 1630.42(c)
14. 8 USC Sec. 1426
15. Reg. Sec. 1630.42(d)
16. Reg. Sec. 1630.46
17. 8 USC Sec. 1426
18. Brownell v. Rasmussen, 235 F. 2d 527 (DC Cir. 1956)
19. Reg. Sec. 1630.46
20. 8 CFR Sec. 215

BOOKS ABOUT CALIFORNIA LAW

AFTER THE DIVORCE by Joseph Matthews. How to modify alimony, child support and custody. $14.95.

BILLPAYERS' RIGHTS by Peter Honigsberg & Ralph Warner. How to handle credit and debt problems. $10.95

CALIFORNIA MARRIAGE & DIVORCE LAW by Toni Ihara & Ralph Warner. Community property, names, children. Includes a sample contract and will. $14.95

CALIF. PROFESSIONAL CORPORATION HANDBOOK by Anthony Mancuso and Peter Honigsberg. Includes all the forms and instructions needed to incorporate a professional business. $24.95.

CALIFORNIA TENANTS' HANDBOOK by Moskovitz, Warner and Sherman. Preventing and solving problems commonly faced by renters. $9.95

CRIMINAL RECORDS BOOK by Warren Siegal. How to get criminal records sealed, destroyed or changed. $12.95

EVICTION BOOK FOR CALIFORNIA by Leigh Robinson (Express). Step by step instructions on how to evict a tenant. Includes all necessary forms. $14.95

FIGHT YOUR TICKET by David Brown. Instructions for contesting a traffic ticket in court. $12.95

HOMESTEAD YOUR HOUSE by Ralph Warner. Forms and instructions for filing a declaration of homestead to protect the equity in a house. $8.95

HOW TO ADOPT YOUR STEPCHILD by Frank Zagone. How to prepare all the legal forms and go through a court adoption procedure for. $17.95

HOW TO CHANGE YOUR NAME by David Loeb and David Brown. How to change your name through the court or the simpler "usage" method. $14.95

HOW TO DO YOUR OWN DIVORCE by Charles E. Sherman. The original "do your own law" book. All forms and instructions for doing your own uncontested dissolution without a lawyer. $12.95

HOW TO FORM YOUR OWN CORPORATION by Anthony Mancuso. All the forms, bylaws, articles, minutes, stock certificates and instructions necessary to form your own small profit corporation. $24.95

NON-PROFIT CORPORATION HANDBOOK by Anthony Mancuso. How to qualify then file all papers necessary to form a non-profit. $24.95

PLAN YOUR ESTATE by Denis Clifford. How to make your will, with information on trusts, taxes and probate avoidance. $15.95

BOOKS FOR PEOPLE IN ALL STATES

ALL ABOUT ESCROW by Sandy Gadow (Express). All the information you need to sell or buy property without a realtor. $10.95

AUTHOR LAW by Brad Bunnin and Peter Beren. Legal aspects of dealing with publishers, co-authors and agents, and lots more. $14.95

BANKRUPTCY: DO IT YOURSELF by Janice Kosel. How to do a Chapter 7 bankruptcy to wipe out all old debts and start over. $14.95

CHAPTER 13 (Bankruptcy) by Janice Kosel. How to develop a court-protected plan to repay your debts over a three-year period. $12.95

DRAFT LAW GUIDEBOOK by R. Charles Johnson. How the new draft registration law works, and what your options are under it. $9.95

EVERYBODY'S GUIDE TO SMALL CLAIMS COURT by Ralph Warner. How to present a small claims case in court, and how to collect your money. $9.95

HOW TO BECOME A U. S. CITIZEN by Sally Abel. Forms and instructions for the naturalization process, with a study guide to U.S. history and government. $9.95

HOW TO COPYRIGHT SOFTWARE by M. J. Salone. How to establish copyright. Common mistakes and how to avoid/correct them. $21.95

LANDLORDING by Leigh Robinson (Express). Getting good tenants, keeping records, maintenance, and what to do when you have problems. $15.00

LEGAL CARE FOR YOUR SOFTWARE by Dan Remer. How a programmer can protect work through trade secret, copyright, patent, contracts, etc. $24.95

LEGAL GUIDE FOR LESBIAN/GAY COUPLES by Hayden Curry & Denis Clifford. Covers buying property, wills, raising children, etc. With sample contracts. $14.95

LEGAL RESEARCH by Steve Elias. A hands-on guide to unravelling the mysteries of a law library, how to find and interpret the law. $12.95

LIVING TOGETHER KIT by Toni Ihara and Ralph Warner. A legal guide for unmarried couples. complete with a living together contract. $14.95

MARIJUANA: YOUR LEGAL RIGHTS by Richard Moller. What the laws are in each state, and how to protect your privacy and property. $9.95

MEDIA LAW by Kathy Galvin. Information about censorship, invasion of privacy, libel, using the Freedom of Information Act, and more. $14.95

THE PARTNERSHIP BOOK by Denis Clifford and Ralph Warner. How to establish a solid, legal partnership, with sample agreements. $17.95

SMALL TIME OPERATOR by Bernard Kamoroff (Bell Springs). How to start and operate your own small business, complete with ledgers and worksheets. $9.95

SOURCEBOOK FOR OLDER AMERICANS by Joseph Matthews. Detailed information on Social Security, Medicare, Medicaid, legal rights, etc. $12.95

START-UP MONEY by Michael McKeever. How to clarify business goals and prepare a business plan and loan package to get financing. $17.95

YOUR FAMILY RECORDS by Carol Pladsen and Denis Clifford. A workbook for recording legal, financial and personal information about you and your family. $12.95

WILLWRITER by Steve Elias and Ralph Warner (Program by Legisoft). A computer disc is included with this manual to guide you through preparing your will. Runs on Apple II, IBM PC, etc. $39.95

AND SOME BOOKS JUST FOR FUN

CALIFORNIA WINE WINNERS by Trudy Ahlstrom and J. T. Devine. A guide to the medal winners in each year's California wine releases. Published every year in November, beginning with 1983. $4.95

HYDRO-STORY by Charles E. Sherman and Hap Brenizer. Entertaining and easy instructions on how to garden without soil--hydroponically. $4.95

MURDER ON THE AIR by Ralph Warner and Toni Ihara. A fast-paced murder mystery set in Berkeley. Time out from all this legal stuff for a little fun. $5.95

29 REASONS NOT TO GO TO LAW SCHOOL by Toni Ihara and Ralph Warner. A cartoon book about what happens to otherwise normal folks when they go to law school. $6.95

UP AND RUNNING by Charles E. Sherman (Ashton-Tate). The stories of 35 entrepreneurs who built the exploding software industry --their successes, failures, risks and rivalries. Personalities behind the power. $15.95

Order Form

QUANTITY	TITLE	UNIT PRICE	TOTAL

Prices subject to change

☐ Please send me a catalogue of your books

Tax: (California only) 6½% for Bart, Los Angeles, San Mateo & Santa Clara counties; 6% for all others

SUBTOTAL _____

Tax _____

Postage & Handling ___$1.00___

TOTAL _____

Name_____

Address_____

_____

☐ I am not on Nolo's mailing list and would like to be. (If you receive the NOLO NEWS you are on the list and need not check the box.)

Send to:

NOLO PRESS
Box 544
Occidental, CA 95465
        or
950 Parker St.
Berkeley, CA 94710